Mari has written an excellent book on what the Old Colony (OC) system really represents from the perspective of her family/grandfather's involvement. The reflection of bondage to man-made rules, both physically and spiritually is what life is all about on the OC colony.

I have personally experienced the "church service in the dark" on Dr. Friesen's yard in Shipyard. This happened on one of my visits to Blue Creek as the Evangelical Mennonite Mission Conference (EMMC) Director of Missions. The buggies arrived once it was dark. In a dimly lit room in a shed, a group of Old Colony families enjoyed a service of songs, preaching, and fellowship. That was the beginning of a new church plant on the colony. Shortly thereafter, a church and school building were constructed close to the Friesen residence, and at that time, serviced by the Blue Creek EMMC.

This book gives a good overview of the Old Colony system and I certainly give my endorsement and encourage reading this book to gain a better understanding of what the Old Colony is all about. Also found here is a snapshot of some of the transitions that have taken place, especially as it applies to the EMMC ministries in Belize, Mexico, and Bolivia.

—Leonard Sawatzky

A Dim Light

Mari Klassen

A DIM LIGHT
Copyright © 2023 by Mari Klassen

Unless otherwise noted Scripture is taken from the Holy Bible, New International Version®, NIV® Copyright ©1973, 1978, 1984, 2011 by Biblica, Inc.® Used by permission. All rights reserved worldwide. • Scripture quotations marked KJV are taken from the Holy Bible, King James Version, which is in the public domain. • Scripture quotations marked (NLT) are taken from the Holy Bible, New Living Translation, copyright ©1996, 2004, 2015 by Tyndale House Foundation. Used by permission of Tyndale House Publishers, Carol Stream, Illinois 60188. All rights reserved.

ISBN: 978-1-4866-2502-4
eBook ISBN: 978-1-4866-2503-1

Word Alive Press
119 De Baets Street Winnipeg, MB R2J 3R9
www.wordalivepress.ca

WORD ALIVE
—P R E S S—

Cataloguing in Publication information can be obtained from Library and Archives Canada.

This book is dedicated to the memory of my grandfather, Bishop Johann M. Loeppky, whose life exemplified a Dim Light still being a Light, leading towards the brightness of the love of Jesus.

ACKNOWLEDGEMENTS

1. FAMILY'S HELP

- Ruben my husband, for his patience and his words of encouragement: "You are destined for the writing of this book..." Your love and supportive prayers truly kept me going.
- daughter Melissa for all your patient help with the technical part of this book
- daughter Maria for walking me through some of the technical parts
- daughter-in-law Jodi for your professional photography for the cover, etc.
- granddaughter Gemma for posing as Marieche (young Grandma) for the cover photo
- My Siblings who all shared their stories. I've also added myself and Henry (deceased) to indicate our placements in the Derksen family.
- John (Johann) Derksen, a draftsman/house designer now retired and living in Warman, Saskatchewan. He has three living children, two grandchildren, and one great-grandson.
- Helen (Helena Derksen) Wiebe, a pastor's wife. She and her husband Richard are now retired and living in Saskatoon. They have

---

five living children, many grandchildren as well as great-grand-children.

- Abe (Abram) Derksen, a retired sign painter living in Vernon, B.C. with his wife Mary. They have three sons and two grandsons.
- Bill (Wilhelm) Derksen, (Dr. of Music) formerly a professor at Providence College near Winnipeg. He and his wife Maryrose are now retired and living in Winnipeg. Their only son Joshua is deceased; their grandson Ocean lives in Winnipeg as well. Thank you, Bill, for also writing the Foreword to this book.
- Henry (Heinrich) Derksen, our brother, who passed away in 2008.
- Mari (Maria) Derksen Klassen (the author). My husband Ruben and I live in Steinbach now; we have four children, all married. We also have nine grandchildren and two step-grandchildren.
- Ike (Isaac) Derksen, a sign painter not completely retired yet. He and his wife Bonnie live in Winnipeg. They have two children and five grandchildren.
- Anne (Anna Derksen) married to Ron Derksen. She was a piano teacher, mostly retired now, living in Winnipeg. They have three daughters and six grandchildren, all of them living in Winnipeg as well

2. Margaret Remple, for helping with the translation of my Aunt Helen's German writings.
3. Leonard Sawatzky, who was the Director of Missions for the EMMC for several years. Thank you for writing an endorsement.
4. Grace Hiebert, who asked me to give my testimony with our Bible Study group which nudged me toward writing this book.
5. The "pastor from Steinbach" who allowed me to quote him in his sermon, not expecting to be recognized. (You know who you are; thank you, I owe you more dates squares!)
6. To Henry and Tina Redekopp for their verification of Aganetha (Nettie)Friesen's testimony.
7. Lastly, thank you to all who prayed for me and encouraged me to "keep writing".

CONTENTS

Foreword

BY BILL DERKSEN

L ike all her siblings and Loeppky cousins, my sister Mari was well aware of the unconditional kindness and generosity of our grandpa. She also came to know that he was the Old Colony bishop, and so was a much-travelled leader, widely known, and loved by all who knew him.

What she learned only in more recent times is that, during his short residency from 1948 to late 1949 in Mexico, he was a controversial leader. It is the origins and extent of the differences between him and the bishop in this country that compelled my sister to research and write about this aspect of our grandfather's life and ministry.

Her interest in writing began with her desire to share with others, in an articulate form, about her faith journeys. This is the subject of a previous book *Another Hannah, 2011.* Prior to this, in 2004, she was inspired to teach English which resulted in her pursuit of a degree, Bachelor of Arts, with a major in TESOL. Teaching English as a second language brought her in touch with Mennonites who had returned to Canada. Her interest in learning more about our roots led her to undertake a trip to Belize in South America where these young people came from. She hoped to get a better understanding of the people she had come to appreciate, and perhaps find some of the cousins we had never known.

This reconnection experience also brought her to more information about the differences between the two bishops. She felt a need to learn more and to write about it.

She immediately realized that a granddaughter's account would easily be, or seem to be, skewed in favour of Bishop Loeppky. Accordingly, she resolved to see both sides of the issue. For example, she read and included excerpts from the writings of Mexican Bishop Isaak M. Dyck, our grandfather's half-brother.

Also included is our grandfather's travelogue of the first trip to Mexico in 1924, as well as the entire pamphlet about him written by the Old Colony treasurer, Abram G. Janzen, who accompanied our grandfather on many of his official trips.

Mari has also interpreted the differences between these two men from her own evangelical faith perspective. What comes through is that Bishop I. M. Dyck believed that a rigorous return to strict teaching and traditions of the church was the reason for leaving Canada and that suffering for one's faith in this life would decrease the likelihood of suffering in the next. Conversely, our grandfather's deep love for his people led him to mitigate, in his preaching and actions, the suffering brought about by this severity. He seemed to have been utterly convinced that the love and grace of God would prevail against the fears of eternal punishment.

A fair bit has been written about Bishop Loeppky; mostly about his important role in the migration of the Old Colony people to Mexico. To all who are interested in the personal sense of mission of this man—his deep love for his people and relentless pursuit of grace and compassion, even to the point of conflict—I recommend *A Dim Light*.

A TRUE STORY I TOLD MY GRANDCHILDREN

Once upon a time, there was a little girl named Marieche (German for "little Mary"). She lived in a small village called Reinland near Osler with the closest city being Saskatoon. She didn't know anything about city life, not the lights or traffic or the hustle and bustle. All she knew was her home in the village which was a house and barn together separated by a summer kitchen. Marieche's job every day was to light the lamps because there was no electricity and no light switches. Lighting the lamps was an important job and you had to do it at the right time. You couldn't start when it was already dark; then you'd have no way to see what you were doing! So, she would hurry and gather the lamps when she noticed the sun starting to go down.

The lamps were very fragile, and you had to be very careful handling them, especially the glass chimneys. They needed to be cleaned because somehow, they always seemed to be sooty and you couldn't see through them. A lamp gives off only a dim light so you want it to be as bright as you can make it. So, Marieche would take a soft cloth and hold it against one end of the chimney. Then she'd blow gently into the other end to make a slight steam. This would make it easier to clean the inside with her cloth until the chimney was clean and shiny. Sometimes she'd end up with a slight ring of soot around her mouth and Mother would tease her if she forgot to clean around her mouth after she'd cleaned the lamps. But the teasing was like a compliment because Mother was very proud of her for doing her job so well.

She also had to make sure there was oil in the lamp so the wick had fuel to "drink". It's like a car needing gas. The wick also had to be trimmed so that it wouldn't create smoke once it was lit. She had to have scissors handy so she could trim it across. Once all this was done, she could light the lamp. Sometimes she had to hurry because it was already almost dark! She knew where the matches were kept but they were almost too high for her to reach. She lit the match and held it to the wick until there was a nice flame. *But* she couldn't leave it this way because it was too dangerous to have an open flame. That's what the chimney was for and she gently slid it into place. Voila! Light in the room at last! It seemed bright to her but actually, it was a very dim light.

However, Marieche had done a good job!

One
A DIM VILLAGE

The light was dim spiritually in our village as well. We grew up in an Old Colony Mennonite setting. Even though the hydro and telephone poles came through our garden, it was considered too worldly to get hooked up to them. Our Mother would have dearly loved the modern conveniences. All the families in this village were Old Colony and we had to be careful to follow the rules. You see, our Mother was Maria Loeppky, daughter of Bishop Johann M. Loeppky. The rules were more in evidence after he died. During the time he was the Bishop, rules were not his priority: he was a man of faith, not rules, as one of my cousins said.

I was born on a farm near Hague, Saskatchewan. My parents were Abram and Maria (Loeppky) Derksen. Before me were 6 others (Johann, Jacob (who didn't live beyond a year due to pneumonia), Helena, Abram, Wilhelm, and Heinrich). Helen had despaired of having a sister so when I was finally born she was given the privilege of naming me. She named me Maria after our mother. I was always called "Marieche" or little Mari and then in our English school simply Mari. A brother and a sister followed and we were a family of eight. My father's family in Hague was quite well to do initially but then the dirty thirties hit and because of co-signing loans for others, not to mention poor farm management; all was lost and we became dependent, so to speak, on the good graces of our other grandfather: Bishop Johann Loeppky.

I was almost 3 when we moved to our grandparent's house in Reinland in 1948. This house had been built by Grandpa. My grandparents lived with us for two weeks. However, they had sold everything and given out their inheritance; our mother received this property (house/barn and 2 acres of land.) They moved to Mexico at the end of November 1948, more than 20 years after the first Old Colony people moved there. When they came back a year or so later, they moved to the village of Newhorst, where he was closer to the Old Colony church.

Reinland was a very small Old Colony Mennonite village of roughly 10 families.

(Note drawings of the village in photo section at the back of the book). My mother grew up in this house and could remember when the thatched roof was replaced with a wooden, shingled roof. A typical house and barn together like we have at the museum in Steinbach Heritage Village here in Steinbach, Manitoba. In fact, if I took you through one of the houses there, I'd be able to identify many items and pieces of furniture that we also had in our home. Items such as the lamp (pictured on the cover) indicate one strong point: no electricity! This was considered "worldly" and definitely had no place in our strong religious community.

The doctrine was essentially having a humble mindset, not considering yourself a "Christian" or "saved" simply because it was too presumptuous: salvation was something you hoped for and along with good works (basically following the church's directives), possibly attained at the end. People often, as best as they knew how, made things right on their deathbeds and yes, hoped for the best. Scriptures such as John 3:16 make it so clear: "For God loved the world so much that He gave His one and only Son, so that everyone that believes on Him will not perish but have eternal life!" These were not emphasized to the congregation, and you were certainly not encouraged to believe this verbatim. It was always only in the "hoping" category. The light was dim indeed.

However, my grandfather Loeppky was more a "man of faith than of rules" as one of my relatives in Belize described him. Let me tell you a bit of his history: When my great-grandmother was seven months pregnant with him, his father met an untimely death in a gruesome accident with his runaway horses. So he never knew his father and when my great-grandmother remarried, the new husband didn't want him.

According to our aunt, he told them that when he was six years old, he was taken to the barn by his stepfather and there experienced a thorough spanking (for what he did not know), whereupon his mother took him by the hand and brought him to his maternal grandparents. He had no siblings; they had died in infancy. After a few years, one of his grandparents died and he was then taken in by an English family, hence he could speak English, play the fiddle, and dance! (So we were told). He only became active in the Old Colony faith in his adult years. At first, he was chosen to be a Forsanger (song leader), then a minister, and eventually a Bishop.

When the Old Colony Mennonites were pressured by the government to give up their German schools and join the English schools, it created a huge turmoil amongst them. Their German schools were based on the catechism and the Bible which were an expression/ teaching of their faith. Forcing the English language was an invasion of their faith and furthermore a broken promise of the government. They had a "priviligum" (agreement) with the government where they had been given permission to have their own schools. But they were now being fined and yes even imprisoned if they failed to send them to the English schools.

It was felt they had no choice but to uproot from their beloved Canada and find a safer haven. "Fight or flight" was always flight for the Mennonites as they are inherently pacifist. And so my grandfather was chosen as one of the delegates to travel to Mexico to "scout out the land" so to speak. He wrote a journal of that trip (printed here in this book) and the end result was that "Bishop Loeppky pleaded with tears in his eyes with the Mexican president for freedom of religion and schools and it was granted, " along with land of course. (a quote from a Mennonite encyclopedia.)

And so, many Old Colonists moved to Mexico along with my grandfather's half-brother who was made a bishop there. The ministerial there set strict guidelines, with intentions of being genuine Old Colony. These "guidelines" quickly became a burden to the newly settled people there and they wanted our kindly grandfather back. However, the people in Canada would be left without a shepherd so to speak, since most of the Old Colony ministers moved to Mexico. (See the writings of Abram G. Janzen, included further on in this book.)Bishop Loeppky spent many years leading the flock left behind in Canada, electing many other clergy to help him.

However, as mentioned, Altester (Bishop) Loeppky eventually decided to move to Mexico as well. And so in 1948, (pictures in photo section at the back of the book) he went, taking more Mennonites, along with some Kleingemeinde from Manitoba. These Kleingemeinde had no qualms about rubber tires (which were banned by the leadership in Mexico) so that was one strike against our grandfather. The other was his more evangelical-type preaching which his half-brother in Mexico was not going to allow. In fact, he warned the people of excommunication if they would so much as go and listen to his preaching. Bishop Loeppky tried to meet with his half-brother Bishop Dyck, but he was unavailable.

In his journal of his trip to Mexico, our grandfather writes of the initial stages of his journey, how he met with many loved ones and friends who prayed with the group and hosted them as the delegates gathered themselves together from both Saskatchewan and Manitoba. In Manitoba were his family, his Dyck half-brothers and sister as well as his mother. He especially wanted to see his half-brother Isaak Dyck who was also a minister. Brother Isaak came to meet him and, "We embraced dearly, and shook hands. I thanked them heartily for coming..." Here we see our grandfather's deep regard for his half-brother. Further on he continues: "Brother Isaak Dyck and I stayed the night at the Heide's, and this was the first time in our lives that my brother and I stayed together and talked a long time. Our hearts were both so bound together, just like David and Jonathan's..."

(How sad that on his later trip to Mexico in 1948 this bond was to be tested and torn apart.) His Mexico experience left him a saddened man. It is said that after he left, the walls of the buildings where he had preached were whitewashed to "wash away his words"!

My grandfather died a few months later, in August of 1950; I was only 5.

We, during the time he was still alive, didn't really experience any harsh restrictions because Bishop Loeppky was not about rules and excommunicating members of the church. He was more about the heart and how we reflected our faith in being kind and helpful; not in judgement.

In the coming chapters, I will be quoting from my siblings with comments from myself as well.

Two

THE BISHOP IS PREACHING

This story is from brother Bill as he experienced an Old Colony worship service:

DER FRIEDE DES HERREN

At an Old Colony service, as many as three hymns were sung at the beginning, each with as many as a dozen stanzas, sung very slowly. For a 7-year-old boy, this was gruelling! Nevertheless, I accompanied my parents to church rather often, to please my mother.

During this extensive, agonizing session, I thought about one thing. As I looked around, I suspected that everyone thought the same thing: what are the chances that the presiding minister-the one leading the ministerial team into the sanctuary from the door on the left—would be Bishop Johann Loeppky? Not that good, actually. There may have been as many as six ministers with four or five churches to be serviced in rotation. No one, not even my mother, who was the bishop's daughter, knew the rotation plan. (It would be wrong to base church attendance on which minister would be leading.) So we were left to hope—through all those endless stanzas.

When finally, after the last hymn, and a suspenseful pause, that door on the left opened, many a bowed head turned upward to see: it was, indeed, the beloved bishop! Taking a few paces into the sanctuary to ensure that the other two ministers were also in, he paused, and in his well-known, rich, deep voice, half singing, half speaking, he intoned "Der Friede des Herren sei mit uns alle. Amen." (The peace of Christ be with us all.)

Full of inexplicable joy, I looked around and was, nevertheless, disappointed to see a number of handkerchiefs come out to dry away tears. Why tears?!

There wasn't going to be much else to the service; the sermon had to be in high German.

Once home, I asked my mother about those handkerchiefs—could they have been tears of joy because he was known for emphasizing the peace, the love, the mercy, and the compassion of God? She replied, "Bill, you have that exactly right!"

I have no doubt that most of the congregants had an experience much like mine: we didn't actually need to understand the sermon. (It was in high German while our everyday language was low German). Bishop Loeppky *was* the message. In a religious milieu in which innumerable rules, many of them unrealistic, were regularly touted, there was much spiritual anxiety. Have we done enough? Will there be mercy for the many compromises? In this community of constant "fear and trembling" came peace and hope from an unlikely source—the head of the entire denomination. Bishop Johann Loeppky was to all the highest human representation of "der Friede des Herren" (the peace of Christ).

And it was among us.

Three
MORE SIBLING MEMORIES

JOHN:

"Grandpa was one of the nicest people I've ever met. He was selfless and had a good spirit. I remember it was dark when we moved to Reinland to live in our grandparents' house. I was helping unload the wagon; I had a little lantern with two batteries and wore it around my neck so I could use my hands to work. Grandma thought that was too worldly! Another time when our grandparents still lived with us, I got into trouble with grandma: I was intrigued with the train running through our village and now I could hear it again! Never mind that it was already late at night, I tried to wake up Helen so she could share in this train experience. Grandma saw this and gave me a resounding slap! Our mother came and admonished her, letting her know it was not *her* place to discipline her children!"

When asked about his spiritual experience, John had this to say: "I was going to the LaBasse school in Reinland. Our teacher Mr. N. had his Bible open and was explaining to us that we should let Jesus come into our hearts. So I did that one day and the next day as I reflected on it, I affirmed that yes that is what I wanted to do. Then it hit me "like a ton of bricks." I felt His sweet presence with me. As I grew older I often sinned and was worried I had lost my salvation so I asked my parents but they reassured me. Later I was baptized but not in the Old Colony church. My girlfriend was in the Bergthaler Mennonite church."

It was a good thing our grandfather had done away with the rule of excommunication if you changed to the Bergthaler church. I did, however, hear rumblings that our John's name was now stricken off the Lamb's Book of Life. (Only in some people's opinion!)

HELEN:
Grandpa lost his first wife (our mother's mother) when she didn't convalesce the full ten days after having a baby as was the custom in those days. She died as a result which he blamed himself for. So whenever our mom had a baby he would come all the way to Blumenthal in his horse and buggy to make sure mom stayed in bed the full ten days. He told our father to make sure she didn't get up sooner. She said he always also brought something to celebrate the new child.

She says, "One time I stayed with the grandparents for a week. It was quiet and I did a lot of chattering, to the point where Grandma asked me to 'tone it down'. I pouted the rest of the day and wouldn't speak at all but was happy to do the few chores I was given. At the end of the day, I was complimented on having curtailed my chattering."

She also said our step-grandma was actually very nice.

Her spiritual experience was similar to that of John and Abe: As with John and Abe, Mr. N the schoolteacher had a great impact in his daily exhortations along with the devotional he gave every morning, imploring the students to be saved. This was what her hungry heart wanted and she did pray that prayer. However, she says her experience was fragmented with doubt; can I be born again today and yet sin the next day? She asked Mom about it and was reassured that she didn't need to do this every day; once was sufficient. She asked Mom for an English Bible and she got one for Christmas! Even at that, she didn't experience all the amazing joy she saw several years later in her husband when he found the Lord. At first, however, Richard says he was discouraged by a verse in James 2:10: "For the person who keeps all of the laws except one is as guilty as a person who has broken all of God's laws." He felt there was no hope for him. He saw joy and excitement in our brother John with whom he had many arguments about religion, citing this and similar doubts that Helena had experienced. John graciously ceded the arguments but prophetically declared one day Richard also would experience the Lord and everything would make sense. This is exactly what happened, accompanied by joy and confidence in his salvation. (This confidence was hard to find among the Old Colony people.)

Together, however, they experienced much persecution from the church leaders, even being told to leave the church premises. They persevered in their new-found faith, however, and later Richard went on to Bible school and became a minister in several Evangelical churches, including one in Mott, N. Dakota.

ABE:

"Grandpa was very loving and compassionate. He would come to visit our farm in his black one-horse buggy with the umbrella shade on it. Often, he would give me and my younger brother Billy each a nickel (a lot of money in those days). Grandpa would be known to also sacrifice his own plate of food when it looked like there might not be enough for everyone. When our family moved into their house in Reinland, Grandpa was also very generous in many ways."

BILL:

"It was Friday, just home from school. This is undoubtedly an 8-year-old's best possible time of the week - the longest stretch of the weekend ahead.

"Mom reminded us all: 'Don't forget there's the funeral tomorrow and you all have to go.' This was a downer, of course, but then I had never known Annie. And to be relieved, after who knows how long, of the pain of leukemia was, as everyone said, a relief.

"But mother continued: 'Abe and Henry, you'll need to go to the store to be fitted with new shoes. Bill's are still OK.' At this, I created a terrible scene. Crying, yelling, shouting unfair, etc. At some point I realized that everyone was playing outside - only Mother and I were left in the summer kitchen, and she was paying no attention to me.

"I became almost overwhelmed by how utterly pathetic I had been. And how fortunate that only mom knew! Just then I heard a deep voice from the next room calling my name: 'Villy'.

"My mind raced - I should have known that for a funeral in our village, the bishop - my Grandpa - would officiate and, therefore, stay at our place. As I walked slowly towards the door, I recalled that this man had famously never been known to be angry. It was most disturbing to think that now, one of his grandsons, had finally pushed him over the edge! But one could not ignore his directive, 'Come.'

"I entered the room but stayed at the door. Whatever he had to say could be done at this distance. But no, he motioned for me to come right to him. When I got there, he put me on his right knee. With his left hand, he reached into the pocket of his priestly smock, then put into my hand exactly enough money for 'a Coke and an O'Henry bar.' Right then this represented to me more joy than all the shoes in the village store! On my way out he said, 'Let's keep this between you and me. The other children don't need to know. But be sure to do all the chores that your mother wants you to do.'

"In later years I told myself that if my grandpa, a mere human after all, could show this much grace, would God show any less? What had happened essentially was that when I was utterly ridiculous, he called, but didn't even mention my 'sin' because he was completely preoccupied with one thing - blessing me."

In his journal of his trip to Mexico, our grandfather gives insight as to his source of Light in a prayer he prayed: "When all our tears that we for Thee have shed, but by Thee are written in heaven, that I through Grace can reach where all Yours are, who have come through great troubles.

"Who have washed their clothes and have made their clothes bright in the Blood of the Lamb, O Lord, may I now and forever, pray, erase through Jesus' Blood, and through Grace, fare well with me." (This is a translation from his original High German version and some of his actual meanings may have "gotten lost in the translation" as they say.)

He goes on to say: "In this world, I can earn nothing, even if I have made a trip, I am still only dust and ashes, yes, a sinful person, but through the promise of Thy dear Son, that nobody shall be lost, instead He will gather us all, I dare to pray, Lord through Grace, go not with me in judgement and cast me not from thee, then my emotions of fear will break."

On the train going to Mexico, they encountered a lady going to see a doctor in Rochester as she was sick with cancer. She had related her many hardships and her earnest prayers to God to "embrace her and through grace help her." It was a great help, on our important journey, to remember how much she had endured, and this gave us faith and hope. Many tears were shed by her in a short time on the train. To God, who is a precious Friend, and who so gladly wants tears, at least those that come from a true believer, who come to Him through hunger and longing for His Grace. Hopefully, He will enter her name in the everlasting testament, and for all her sorrows and suffering through grace be rewarded. In the scriptures, flowing tears are like sheaves. Tears show that a person's heart has softened and that the Lord plans to enter into one's heart and does so in a person following the holy trail by His Son. In this manner is a person born again through the Holy Seed, and one becomes a much better person after enduring sadness and hardships. Yes, my beloved, after repentance, everything is important. One is spiritually raised from the dead and works to serve the living God. As Jesus said, "The words I speak are Spirit and Life".

Four

A FLICKERING FLAME

The next bishop, however, was somewhat aligned with the leadership in Mexico. So our family was closely watched. You see, we didn't fit the mould. Our brothers liked musical instruments and played them well. They even had a half-hour radio program and called themselves "The Country Playboys," having no idea what that actually meant. They were very naive. For to them it only meant "country boys who play instruments"! We would sit by that radio as it grew quieter and quieter, so very proud of our big brothers, hoping the battery would last till the end of the program!

Our big brothers also went off to the big city to start working with my mother's warnings of "sinful women, etc." following them. What she wasn't prepared for was them coming home full of joy and endless talk of being saved and born again. Words that were tantamount to blasphemy in an Old Colony home! There were many arguments but we younger ones listened to what they were saying; we were hungry. Our dim little heart lamps were searching for Jesus, the Light of the world. And when my brothers left behind some tracts (which was a thing in those days, it seemed), I followed the "instructions" on "how to be saved" in this tract and gave my heart to Jesus at the age of 12 I believe. I can't say I had any big experience but I knew I wanted to walk the Christian life. So I started talking to my friends about it and that was the beginning of strength and assurance of salvation. Several of my schoolmates also gave their hearts to Jesus but all with relative hesitancy because we were, after all, surrounded by Old Colony disapproval. Canadian Sunday School Mission regularly came to our school encouraging us to memorize Bible verses which most of us did to the max. Our reward was Christian fiction books, the Danny Orliss series, etc. I memorised them all and could have gone to camp but that was not allowed to. DVBS also was not allowed simply because it had never been done before.

I remember asking for a Bible for Christmas and it seemed to be keenly noted by our mother. I felt she understood where I was at spiritually and come Christmas, sure enough, there was a beautiful new Bible for me. I faithfully read it every night, some chapters in the Old Testament and some in the new. One night I was going to forego my Bible reading as I was feeling rather sick. Mother, however, noticed this and encouraged me to read it anyway. I did so and learned a valuable lesson: don't underestimate the rewards of hardship if endured for the sake of godliness.

Singing was another thing that lifted our spirits in school. In fact, our little one-room school won the choir award 3 years in a row The teacher himself couldn't really sing but he had a clarinet and diligently taught us the songs. My older sister taught me to sing alto before I even went to school. And although I've had voice lessons since, I'm comfortable as an alto. I would listen to Back to the Bible mostly for the singing and they sent you a free songbook upon request. Their songs were new to me, but I would guess at the title as they started singing and follow along, learning the melody by following the notes by intervals. (I do that to this day even though my brother taught me music theory in Bible school!) But I'm jumping ahead. My second cousins lived at one end of the village, and they also enjoyed singing. We would always sing on their veranda, belting out our harmonies for the whole village to hear. All this really helped me grow in my Christian walk.

The best times were when my brothers would take us along to their church: friendly people (most of them also our second cousins). Anyways, the services were full of joyful singing and encouraging, uplifting sermons. We knew our mother got criticized for us "wandering off" to another church. We as the younger ones needed to respect that and so our older brothers went without us. But oh, how I prayed that God would someday let me be in a church like that! It felt like heaven!

Five

BURNING THE MIDNIGHT OIL

Miraculously, I was able to go to high school. I had been praying all through grade 8 but thought the best that could happen would be taking grade 9 by correspondence. High school also was not allowed (higher learning would take you further away from the Lord/church). And mother had been waiting for me to finish school so I could be more of a help around the house. My older sister had long since been married with 3 little ones in a small town about 10 miles away. However, without me knowing, my two brothers (Abe and Bill) went to bat for me, buying my books and doing research on the possibilities. Apparently, for the first time ever, the school bus went right by our place! What a surprise when my mother revealed all this to me. Everyone seemed to know I was not one of those who were dying to get out of school as soon as I turned 15! God heard my prayer. High school was a new and scary experience for this very shy girl; I didn't know anyone. But almost immediately I was befriended by two girls, Deanna and Marie, who stuck with me all through high school. There were at least 30 in our grade 9 class (that's how big my one-room school had been!) but I worked very hard, keeping the midnight oil burning (literally) trying to hurry before my dad would remind me I was using up costly kerosene with our bright mantel lamp. My mother had to sacrifice the help I would have been if I'd been home, and she asked me occasionally if I'd stay home. Mostly I didn't but at the beginning of June, we both had our reward.

Because of my good attendance and high marks, I was one of 5 out of our class of 30 grade 9 students who were exempted from all eight provincial exams and finished early. As I came off the bus and into the garden where my mother was working, she noticed all my books and asked what was going on. I teased her by saying I had quit school which made her very upset! After all the sacrifices she had made! I quickly told her the truth: I had finished early due to high marks and good attendance. So now I could be the help she deserved.

For several years, especially in my early teens, I felt that Mother was disappointed in me. I was a new believer and wanted so badly to go to church with my brothers, to that joyful place! However, Mother had been warned to keep a tighter rein on us younger ones seeing how she lost the older ones to this other church. I somehow sensed this but was too immature to keep my arguments to myself. She was under a lot of pressure as a Bishop's daughter, to tow the Old Colony line. That summer, however, we had a wonderful time working together. Those are precious memories.

And we had a wonderful summer, no more arguments about the other church etc. In fact, as we sat down to Faspa one Sunday afternoon, my brother-in-law said: "I am so happy to know that if I'd die today, I would go to heaven because of what Jesus has done for me," I groaned, thinking, "Oh no, not again!" But my mother surprised us with gentle tears, saying, "I know what you are saying, and I can say that as well…" What rejoicing in my heart; our mother was "on the same page" and perhaps had been all along? Just not with our terminology.

Six

A NIGHT OF DARKNESS

B ut then something tragic happened that summer that changed our lives forever and I was not home at the time it happened.

We younger ones took turns staying at my married sister's house for a week during the summer. Usually, Dick and Helen would come on a Sunday and take us along. It was my turn and I had so looked forward to this week. But they did not come. Remember we didn't have a telephone to contact them. And so, on Monday I helped mom with the usual: laundry, etc. At the end of the day, they showed up! I was so happy. We had a lovely time singing together; Mom even had some requests (these were *not* songs from the OC Gesangbuch (songbook)) until it was time to leave. It seemed Mom didn't share the enthusiasm I had for me to go back with them. I said we had done the heavy work for the week and she agreed. She was very vague but in the end allowed me to go, giving us hugs and waving goodbye. (This was quite unusual and we remarked on it as we left).

I had a wonderful week at my sister's as always— until Friday night. I was sharing a bed with my little nephew and he was saying his night-time prayers, "If I should die before I wake, I pray the Lord my soul to take." I felt a stab of foreboding in my spirit but then we all went to sleep peacefully. Until the phone jarred us awake at 2 AM. It was my dad calling from the neighbour's (they were not OC and they had a phone), saying mom was not responding! Apparently, I screamed all the way to the little dark village of Reinland, saying "Mom will be okay, right?" She just fainted. My sister said not a word and this added to the sense of foreboding. When I saw my younger brother and sister waiting for us on the porch in complete silence, I made another feeble effort: if Mother had died, wouldn't they be crying their eyes out? But they couldn't; they were in shock! The truth became very evident as we saw our mother lying motionless on the bed. Our older sister was very sad but knew to be strong for us and her little children as well. Village women came and sat in the room, more as a duty of "wake" than to comfort to us. I was conspicuous because I had rollers in my hair (Helen had given me a perm). Very bad. When I started crying, I was quickly shushed up so I went outside to pour out my grief to my Father in Heaven. He gave me a song which calmed me, these words from the last verse of HE LEA-DETH ME: "Even death's cold wave I will not flee, since God through Jordan leadeth me...." Gently showing me that I could put my trust in Him. He would lead me and take care of me. The doctor came and tried to assess the reason why she died but other than possibly her heart, (she was on high blood pressure pills) there was no definite conclusion. I felt so guilty thinking she must have worked too hard and if I had been home to help her, she might not have died.

My younger sister came to her just as she was dying: (she might not have if I'd been home). Let me explain: Mom always made sighing and moaning noises in her sleep. My older sister had told me this long ago and my dad who was right beside her, never noticed anymore. But my younger sister had never heard it and nobody had ever told her not to worry. So when she heard Mother moaning, she got up and went to see what was wrong. She heard Mother give a deep sigh and although she tried to rouse her, she only woke Dad up. He expressed annoyance that she was disturbing mother. All too quickly he realized the terrible truth: she was gone.

ISAAC:
"It was the darkest day of my life: August 5th, 1961. In the middle of the night, our family realized that our mother had died. Dad had phoned

Dick and Helen and they contacted other family members in the city. He informed the village storekeeper, waking him by tapping on their windows.

"Dad realized that we should also notify the local preacher. This is where I sprang into action, with my sister Anna, to start the old truck to drive to the preacher's house to inform him of the tragedy. I am now in my element—being tasked with driving on purple tractor gas, a license plate that still says 1957, no brakes and being under-aged to drive. So we begin this ominous journey, by putting my heel onto the accelerator, the toe on the long spring-loaded starter shaft, the left hand on the choke and this worn-out Fargo motor comes to life. Now comes a series of left-hand turns, the first of which is to navigate past a dozen or so cars, uncharacteristically scattered across our yard. What does it take, for the many cars that usually drive past our house, to finally come into our yard? Does someone have to die?

"Two more left turns, and then a right turn onto that long narrow driveway to the preacher's house. All is dark and quiet but for the two headlights and the persistent honking announcing that something has gone terribly wrong. Surely now, the preacher will talk to us. But instead, it is his wife who comes to the door. She asks 'What is wrong?' Anna says, 'Our Mother has died.' While the preacher's wife is processing that, I keep looking to the window where a dark figure is reluctantly moving towards the door. We drive back home—our task is complete.

"The preacher comes later that morning, talks with our Dad briefly, and quietly slips away. How we longed for the gentle and compassionate presence of our Grandfather.

"I personally, at age three, have two memories of our grandfather.

"One: sitting on his lap receiving peppermint candy, and two: the occasion of his funeral—sitting on the tailgate of the hearse-truck, the coffin behind me and my mother beside me."

He also shares his faith story:

"I came to faith through my Grandfather (his life and legacy) and my parents at an early age. We had weekly church services in our home with scripture reading, prayer and hymn singing, all in High German. I came to a clearer understanding of faith through the English Gospel songs as presented by the local public school teachers at La Basse Elementary School in Reinland, Sask. This was a more personal emphasis. I then attended an evangelical revival meeting where the evangelist invited us, with heads bowed and eyes closed to a special prayer of confession and acceptance of Jesus as personal Saviour. I now stated with the Apostle Paul, 'I am crucified with Christ: nevertheless I live; yet not I but Christ lives in me: and the life that I now live in the flesh I live by faith of the son of God, who loved me and gave Himself for me. ' (Gal. 2:20, KJV). A further step of faith was baptism and church membership a few years later.

"Other decisions of change were made. One day at work, where, after several years of listening to talk radio with Peter Warren, I crossed the floor to change the station to Peter Gzowski. Better music and a wider point of view. That's where I learned about Lister Sinclair introducing us to Hector Berlioz and "Symphony Fantastique". This most beautiful music was heard on my red K-car radio driving home on the North Perimeter just as I overshot the McPhillips Street overpass. This music was also the featured work many, many years later at a Hilton Head Island symphony concert, conducted by John Russell with a Canadian connection. We were sitting in the very front pew in that Presbyterian Church when I noticed his very shiny black shoes and bright red shoelaces. After the concert, he turned around to us and engaged in a pleasant conversation about Canada.

"On our way home through the Great Smoky Mountains, we happened upon the Blueridge Parkway—the slowest way home. After three hours of a hopeless traffic jam, we decided to take a break, stopped at a Bible Store and bought a large print traditional translation for $5.00, with the words of Jesus in red. Despite years of Sunday School, Bible School and countless religious discussions, many of the difficult questions of the day could not be adequately explained. So I started reading only the red letters to see, "What did Jesus say?"

"Well, maybe something like: 'Worship God and follow me, even unto death'?

"So I have decided to follow Jesus, in my red-laced shoes—no turning back."

ME, MARI:

For years I carried this terrible guilt of not being home to help; perhaps our mother would not have died. Until one day in a counselling session with the Freedom in Christ husband and wife team from Winnipeg. She was praying for me about this and I sensed God saying to me, 'That was not your work'. And even more impactful the realization that: If I *had* been home, I would have prevented little Anna from getting up to investigate Mom's moaning and we wouldn't have found her till morning. My guilt would have been unbearable! Our God is so gracious in His ways, I am so thankful. Apparently, according to my brother-in-law, we Derksens do "guilt" well and that is *not* a compliment!

I was 15 when this happened; Ike was 13 and little Anna was only 11. My brother Henry was 17, and not in school anymore. He was away working on a farm at the time of Mom's death.

A bit more about Henry: He would be considered mentally weak academically. I surpassed him in school, much to my embarrassment. However, he had a brilliance that was amazing: he built a miniature threshing machine that really worked. It was his pride and joy!

In school one day, the teacher announced we'd be making pinwheels to stick out on the lawn and watch them spin in the breeze. He was explaining the pattern when Henry piped up: "That's not going to work." He said it in a subdued voice but it irritated the teacher nonetheless! So, while everyone was imitating the teacher's instructions, Henry quietly made his "the right way". The pupils proudly displayed their pinwheels on the lawn. However, they did not spin. Henry's was the only one spinning!

We had a big party two weeks before his actual September 4th birthday when he turned sixty-five. Somehow, intuitively, we had prepared a photo album for him which he deeply appreciated. Birthday cake, singing together (with instruments accompanying of course) made this time very special for him. The Derksen Trio sang "O Happy Day" for him and he said, "This is a happy day!" Henry died just days before his 65th birthday and we all miss him so much. He had technical ingenuity that amazed us all. I'm sure he would have mastered the computer world if he had lived long enough! He died September 15th, 2008.

Back in 1961 when our mom died: The night after she died, Bill stayed and had devotions with us. But he chose the verse which said: "Always be full of joy in the Lord. I say it again- Rejoice..." (Philippians 4:4)! Whoa...that's surely not expected at a time like this! But he said something that impacted me for many years to come; even to this day... God *is* expecting us to rejoice because we can trust Him to take care of us. We should be honoured that He trusts *us* to look to Him in a difficult time like this.

Were we up to the challenge? It was the only way... to look to Jesus, He would see us through. Little Anna just knew that Jesus was coming soon: this was just too terrible. We also prayed together, wondering whether it was okay to go to the evangelical church now; we wanted to continue honouring our mother in what she had wanted. The doctor had left behind some sleeping pills; I took half of one but little Anna said no. We slept well that night and Anna shared with us a dream she had had which really impacted her and the rest of us as well. She had seen Mom in heaven clapping her hands and smiling as she saw us go to the evangelical church. We knew we had our answer!

The funeral was difficult. It was in the Old Colony church of course but there was no real sympathy shown. We were on display on the stage where the Vorsaenger (song leaders) usually sat, so everyone could see the shame and hurt when the minister blamed us for our mother's untimely death, saying we had grieved her by going off to another church etc.

Now life had to go on but it was so hard. I was the work organizer and perhaps a bit bossy which was met with resentment from the younger ones. Dad was in his own world of grief while we were in need of help and support. Helen stepped in to help me organize our lives. I was hoping she would scoop us all up and take us to Warman (where they lived), because life was going to be just too hard. But we tried to regroup ourselves and work together: cooking and baking with a wood-burning stove, cleaning the house and all the other chores in a no-electricity house, all without our kind Mother overseeing us. We all dreaded going into the living room where she had died in her sleep. Coming home to an empty house was also very eerie: Mom just wasn't there and Dad usually escaped to the village store to avoid loneliness. An empty house equals empty hearts.

The bridges were burnt behind us as far as the Old Colony Church was concerned. Dad continued going to the Old Colony church but the rest of us felt released now to go to my brother's church. And that is where the real healing and support came: they would pick us up on Friday nights for youth and choir practice. Sunday morning the Sunday school teacher would come and get us, sometimes we were invited for lunch and returned home later. We lived for the weekends! A whole new world! A world of love and acceptance, joyful singing and wonderful truths of assurance from the Word of God! A world of Light! I realized it was the answer to my prayers, but it saddened me that it came at such a cost! I was asked to give a testimony, but I couldn't finish because of this realization! It was too soon to share and we just received the love and drank in everything God had for us. (We remembered also, how our mother would always be found kneeling in prayer for a lengthy time beside her bed in the living room (there was no separate bedroom for the parents). Was she praying for us, her children? Perhaps that is why we all found our way to the Light in the midst of seeming darkness.)

In our little village, however, we were very lonely as we were mostly ostracized after the minister's words. There was very little support shown to us in the village. When it came time to do the annual pig-butchering, I was very anxious about my role. The villagers would always come and do the work together. The men would work outside, cutting up the pig while the women cooked a huge meal for everyone. They also did much of the finer work such as getting the intestines ready for making sausages. (This was always my job.) But now I would have to do so much more and I was terrified. Would I have to be in charge in the house, organizing the work in the kitchen, etc.? I stayed home from my beloved high school that day, terrified of the expectations. Dad had not enlightened me and I had no idea as to what to do.

To my great surprise and delight my Loeppky aunties from Newhorst came and took over. There was no judging or shaming me for knowing next to nothing. (Or for going to high school and that "other church"!) They knew what to do and did it with great joy, giving me familiar jobs and most importantly, they gave me loving acceptance! I felt elated and "light-hearted" at the end of the day; the work all got done and I had not messed it up with my ignorance!

But we had our daily struggles. Our dad had spent 6 months in the mental hospital before our mom's death (he became obsessed with the unfairness of the loss of our farm, etc.) to the point of not being able to function. He was doing very well when he came back, but now we were concerned about his mental health slowly deteriorating again.

During this time, close to Christmas, my brother remembers us being invited by friends to hear a program in Osler, a nearby town. We were getting rides with them. I vaguely remember this. Isaac said that one song they sang was "Star of the East" which impacted our dad so much that he couldn't stop talking about this when we got home. I was able to remember it enough to get us to try singing it, but probably not exactly like we heard it. And that was the beginning of our Derksen Trio (Ike, Anne and I). We had come through a difficult winter but in the spring, God gave us a desire to sing. With that came the beginning of healing...God is so faithful.

Some of my siblings also share memories of that time:

JOHN (the oldest and already married, living in Saskatoon):
"I was very devastated to hear of mom's death. But Mom deserved a better life so this was a blessing to her...heaven was her reward. I felt guilty though for sharing a stupid joke with one of our cousins at the funeral. I remember how Mom could make everything interesting. She also made good food out of almost nothing."

I (Mari) would add that she would get clothes from the Salvation Army and take them apart. I helped her by holding the garment while she cut the threads in the seams with a razor blade. These she would alter to make suitable and wearable clothes. She never let anything go to waste; a very resourceful woman.

ABE:
"I felt bad that I hadn't seen her in over a month. I had bought my first VW but it wasn't working, not road-worthy for longer trips. I wanted to

trade it off but that hadn't happened yet. I called the police and the coroner. I went with the policeman in his car. The coroner was right behind us as we drove to Reinland. We directed the policeman to turn right after a hill. It was a sharp turn and unexpected for the coroner which caused him to smash into the policeman's car. We got there a little shaken up."

He goes on to share his faith story: "There was a Mr. F. that came to the schools, sharing Bible stories via flannel graph. He had such a burden for the Old Colony children that he would occasionally pick them up in his '28 Plymouth for a picnic. He had his guitar and would sing songs like 'Jesus Loves the Little Children' and 'Precious Jewels'. It was the first time I heard a guitar being played and it stirred up the love for music in me.

"You could feel the love and gentleness through this man. It was as if an angel came to give us something special.

"Then in the school in Reinland, the teacher, Mr. N. shared the gospel after which I prayed to receive Jesus into my heart. And it worked! Although I had received the Lord, there wasn't really a chance to grow spiritually in the Old Colony church, but I listened to Back to the Bible which really helped me.

"Music became my passion and my older brother John and younger brother Billy were equally on board as we joined up with bands that got us playing for dances and even the radio! Very exciting times. Eventually, things started spirally downwards and when the band broke up, I realized God was speaking to me about my spiritual life. I told Billy I was quitting the band and giving it all up. He stayed a little longer but then quit as well. We looked for a church to attend and eventually ended up at the Rudnerweidner (also known as the Evangelical Mennonite Mission Conference). Here my faith came alive again. It's also where I met my wife Mary. This was during 1957, I believe.

"We came home some weekends and wanted to share our newfound joy in our faith. However, Mother didn't understand what was happening. I regret not going slower to show her what it really meant. When I did finally take the time to gently explain it all to her, I sensed that she began to understand and she approved, even coming to my baptism in this new church. She was under a lot of stress though, being pulled in two directions. (She was, after all, the Bishop's daughter and needed to keep her children in the Old Colony church!)"

ANNA (Anne now):
"From my earliest days of memory, I was taught the stories of Christmas and Easter and also enjoyed other Bible stories taught at home and school. When I was around 8 years old, my older siblings had many discussions with my parents, sharing the joy of their personal faith journeys and doctrinal beliefs which had become increasingly important. I listened and became more curious.

"When I was 10, I stayed with my older brother John and his wife Betty. I asked her why Jesus had to die and she shared her thoughts on making faith personal as we read in John 3:16 "For God so loved the world that He gave His only begotten Son, that whosoever believes on Him will not perish, but have everlasting life." My part was to confess my sin and receive Jesus as my Saviour through faith. I eagerly did this when I prayed before I went to sleep that night and consider this my "born again" experience as we read in John 3:3 "Jesus replied, 'Very truly I tell you, no one can see the kingdom of God unless they are born again.'"

"This was followed by overwhelming thoughts of heaven which I shared with my sister-in-law the next morning. This experience has been an anchor in my faith which I have happily reaffirmed through baptism when I was 19 as well as other times throughout my life. My faith is my treasure and nurturing it through Scripture is a great blessing.

"When I was 11, on August 4, I had a restless day; my sister was not home and things were rather boring in our small village. I tried to have a nap with my mom but was dismissed as I interfered with hers.

"When I went to bed, I was disturbed by a foreboding feeling and told my mom 'I can't sleep." She responded, 'Just think about beautiful things.' A few hours later I heard her groan and gasp for breath and then...silence. Her life had just ended and mine was about to change.

"The kindness and goodness of my siblings and others was overwhelming and helped me learn to rely on Jesus to direct my life and help me find my way. I have experienced His presence and blessings

27

significantly, realizing personally that 'all things work together for good', as we read in the Bible. I'm so blessed to have had a mom who nurtured faith and all values kind and good. I don't remember hugs or "I love you"s. I do remember feeling I was loved and cared for.

"I missed having my husband and children meet and get to know her and I have also dearly missed having her as my friend in my adult years."

Yes, I echo that sentiment; I talk about my mom a lot, but my husband and children have also never met her.

John Loeppky, a cousin from Warman, Saskatchewan has some memories of our grandfather as well:

"He was very impressive looking in his Priestly clothes. He had a nice buggy and a good horse. For Christmas, we always got a drawing book and a nice new pencil which we greatly treasured. Sometimes we even got coloring books. Mine was a large one with a picture of Gene Autry and his horse rearing up...I really liked that one. I never felt very uplifted when I went to church though; it seemed so depressing."

This cousin also remembers Grandfather as a wise, kind man.

Seven

BRIGHTER LIGHTS

Plans were made to move which we did, almost a year to the date of our mother's death. We moved to the town of Warman right across from our sister's place. Free at last from the confining borders of our old village; life felt so much brighter. Our Evangelical church had already moved there as well so now we could walk to church. We continued in youth and choir and I became a Sunday school teacher. And we continued singing, in churches, even at a huge crusade held in a large Quonset. A whole new world it was. God was teaching us so much. Ike's friend became my boyfriend; they were a singing family as well. I remember their signature song, the chorus was:

> "How beautiful to walk in the steps of the Savior,
> Stepping in the Light, Stepping in the Light
> How beautiful to walk in the steps of the Savior,
> Led in paths of Light."

(*Stepping in the Light*, Words by Eliza Edmund Stites Hewitt, 1880.
Music by William James Kirkpatrick, 1890)

This song aptly described our new Light-filled life as young people. The hardships we had endured since our mother's death did make our hearts soft (as our Grandfather said in his journal) and we were open to learning more about "Walking in the Light". Although my relationship with Ike's friend gradually faded out, Ike and Anne kept up the friendship with this family.

Eight
NEW ENLIGHTENMENT

After graduation and much prayer, I decided to come all the way to Manitoba to the Bible School where Bill had attended: SBI in Steinbach, Manitoba! I came with my cousin to Winnipeg by train and the rest of the way by bus. We received a very warm welcome when we finally got there and I felt so at home. Another whole new world! I was involved in choirs and small singing groups, I lived in a dorm full of fun-loving girls, I didn't have to cook over a wood stove, all my meals were made for me, (I gained weight; I had always been underweight), and I was feeling so very blessed. Bill was right: it is always the right time to rejoice because God is taking care of us.

I so enjoyed studying the Bible full-time: to go into the depths of the Gospels, to go deeper into prayer, to learn about Mennonite history, and to take music courses from my own brother! (I even had the privilege of singing in his choir!) These all helped open my eyes to Christlike maturity and yes "enlightenment"... (Further light).

And then, I didn't mean to; but I met my wonderful husband-to-be (Ruben Klassen) in my second semester. Even though first-year students weren't allowed to date, we were given permission and the best part of my life started. We got engaged during my second year and made wedding plans for August 1966, the wedding to be held back in Saskatchewan; in Saskatoon. We have been married for 57 years, living in Neepawa Man.

most of those years. In my first book, *Another Hannah,* I wrote about our journey of having children; miracle children that is. Read it and like Paul Harvey used to say, you'll get "the rest of the (Ruben and Mari Klassen) story"!

However, a brief summary might be in order: We moved to Neepawa soon after Ruben got his teaching certificate and he started his 25-year career there as an industrial arts teacher. I worked for 25 years as a receptionist, a nurse's aide and Adult Day Program Coordinator. After retirement, I came back to the Bible College here in Steinbach to get my TESOL degree. I taught ESL for 11 years. (The HiLife immigrants needed English).

Nine

FROM DARKNESS TO LIGHT IN BELIZE

THE FRIESENS IN SHIPYARD, BELIZE

In teaching English, I also taught some Mennonites who hailed from Belize, an Old Colony Mennonite settlement in Shipyard. For years I had been burdened by the state of the Mennonites who had moved to Mexico and then subsequently to Belize, Paraguay and Bolivia. I would walk on the highway and pray, sometimes ending up preaching to them in Low German! And here were some Mennonite young people from Belize who had found Jesus by reading the Scriptures on their own. They'd also been excommunicated for doing so and their whole family was shunned because of this.

Their father (David Friesen) has already died but their mother Nettie has shared their story and with her permission, I will share it now:

NETTIE FRIESEN:

"We had 13 children, 2 of which died. We lived in Shipyard, Belize right across from the Old Colony church where we attended. My husband was the doctor and dentist, and assisted with many childbirths. We had a clinic where we saw the patients and a pharmacy to supply them with medicine. We were faithful to the church and thought things were going well.

"However, our three oldest sons were married; there was influence from Canadian youth who had more insights into the scriptures. They had Bible studies together and one by one our sons would come to us excitedly sharing these new truths we had never heard before. I so appreciated them sharing these verses: 1 John 5:13 (NLT) says, 'I have written this to you who believe in the name of the Son of God, so that you may know you have eternal life.' Although I was so excited at the discovery of these verses (the Old Colony teaching is that you cannot know), I nevertheless felt unworthy and couldn't fully receive them. I needed to improve first somehow.

"One Communion Sunday in church, the ministers came in and started with 'Die Friede des Herrn sei mit uns alle,' as usual but after that everything changed! Before the communion was passed around by the elders, the minister said that those who had been drinking and watching TV, etc. could not take communion unless they were sorry for this. Those however who had been part of the Bible Studies, studying the Bible on their own, need not reach out their hand to receive communion. This was a huge shock to my husband and me.

"Our sons had been excited to receive communion after the enlightenment they had received from the Word of God. They were in shock now as it would be denied them. They did not reach out their hands to receive it. The elders came back to one son whom they had missed and asked why he did not reach out his hand. Whereupon the son reminded them that what they said applied to him as well. This was a very difficult day for us. It didn't sit right with my husband.

"So the next day, Monday, he went to speak to the leaders about it. Their answer was that if the boys would promise not to have any more Bible studies on their own, they would be allowed to come back. If they didn't promise this, then they needn't come back.

"It seemed strange to me that the Bishop didn't need to apologize; as if they certainly had done nothing wrong! This was in October of 1998.

"Then in 2001, the elders also excommunicated my husband. He was asked to come to a "Thursday Meeting"(Donnadach) and so he went. I asked if I should come too but he said no even though they had asked for both of us to come. When he arrived, there was no handshake for him and he knew that he would be out. They asked to speak to me as well but my husband said they would have to come to our place to do so.

"They accused me of the same things and would have to excommunicate me as well. I answered with the verses from Romans 8:35: 'Can anything ever separate us from Christ's love?' The Bishop finished the verse… 'Does it mean He no longer loves us if we have trouble or calamity, or are persecuted, or hungry, or destitute, or in danger or threatened with death?' He finished by saying that the mouth can say anything and these verses do not apply; also citing "The apple doesn't fall far from the tree" to show what kind of person you are.

"This was very hurtful and I went back into the house, crying with my head hanging down. However, the New Testament was on the table opened at 1 Peter 4 from which God spoke to me, reassuring me as I read the whole chapter.

"In the end, they did not excommunicate the women in our family although they did a few others. I would have loved it if there had been apologies and things could have been made right: I wanted us to remain Old Colony. My husband saw however that this would not be possible. We had Bible studies in our home and eventually, a new church was built with support from the EMMC. A school was built as well because we no longer had access to the Old Colony School. Although they had warned my husband that as shunned people, he would no longer have a livelihood as a doctor and people would be discouraged from coming to him. However, there really was nowhere else for people to go so they *would* come to him under cover of darkness. We also had land and cattle so we did very well."

Nettie maintained friendship with two ladies, one a sister-in-law and this has always been a blessing to her.

Nettie was also very sincere as she said how forgiveness was very important citing how Jesus had forgiven his tormenters as he died on the cross, saying "Father forgive them for they know not what they do". "I forgive the Old Colony leaders as well for they also know not what they're doing. God will take care of it all."

She struggled with assurance of salvation at times, feeling empty, not completely sure she had been born again. But God spoke to her through the scriptures in Titus 3:4-7 (NLT) "But- when God our Savior revealed His kindness and love, He saved us, not because of the righteous things we had done, but because of His mercy. He washed away our sins, giving us a new birth and new life through the Holy Spirit." From this time on, she has not doubted her salvation.

She is so grateful that all her children are following the Lord and prays that all of them including her 54 grandchildren and 2 great-grand-children will continue walking with Jesus the Truth and the Light. "They cannot depend on me, she says, "Each needs to find Jesus on their own," adding also, that if they hadn't gone through these hardships, they might never have found Jesus. Her story is filled with gratitude to Jesus for His death on the cross and His resurrection wherewith He provided salvation for us all.

God in turn rejoices over us with singing when we seek Him with all our hearts. This family found Jesus the Light and we rejoice with them.

RELATIVES IN BELIZE
My Aunt Anna (Loeppky) and Uncle John Rempel had moved there years ago and I was curious as to any connection. And these Friesen siblings found it: their brother-in-law was my cousin's son! I met him and several of his brothers a few years later. They also had found Jesus after much searching! God is so faithful! I taught them English and they taught me much about the situation of the Mennonites; basically, it was very dark. The teachings/rules set out by my great half-uncle were still being adhered to.

But it was wonderful to hear their redemptive story!

MORE RELATIVES
I'm remembering also a time when we went to visit my cousins in La Crete, Alberta in 2005 I believe. I hardly knew them but asked if we could come. I knew most of them were Old Colony so wasn't sure what kind of reception my husband and I would get because we were definite-ly not Old Colony. What a pleasant surprise! We were warmly welcomed and invited to stay for a few nights at my cousin Nettie and Andrew's place. From here we made the rounds: there were ten in the family! My most urgent reason for coming was to see their mother, my Aunt Helen, my mother's half-sister. She'd had a stroke and wouldn't be able to talk

to me but I wanted to see her so badly: perhaps because my mom died when I was so young and I just wanted to see someone who might look like her! She had been told I was coming but when she saw me we both started crying! She *did* look like my mother. I couldn't help my emotions pouring out; I had not expected this. And later I found out she cried for the same reason: I reminded her so much of her sister Maria, my mom! It was a very powerful experience. Thank you, Helen and Nettie, for facilitating this precious visit.

Most mornings these siblings would get together in a restaurant for coffee or breakfast. One morning it was just the women and I noticed there were others in the group; ladies from the community, some wearing the Old Colony headpiece but others wearing normal clothes like me. I couldn't believe the acceptance and inclusiveness my cousins were showing to these ladies and to myself as well. I asked them about this; one of them related how when they had lived in Rosetown, Saskatchewan, they had been invited to go to Sunday School at an Evangelical church nearby. Here they learned that they needed to accept Jesus into their hearts and believe He died for them. This they did with full approval and even encouragement from their parents. Ah, I understood: the same accepting heart as our grandfather! They also shared how when their mother was growing up, she had seen a coat in the catalogue that she really wanted. But Grandmother said no. Grandfather asked to see what coat she had been looking at and overrode Grandmother's no with a yes!

We left on the day of our anniversary and Nettie gave me a lovely quilt which I use almost daily when I take my nap!

Ten

GREAT DARKNESS

We actually went to Belize a few years later, first to Spanish Lookout where the Kleingemeinde had settled. There was a wonderful EMMC church (Evangelical Mennonite Mission Conference). I was very moved, thinking this is how my Grandfather would have wanted it to be. I knew it was very dark at Shipyard and we would be going there for most of our stay. So I was asking God, "What can I do?" I'm not a preacher; I wouldn't be able to preach there. However, when I got there, the radio pastor of the mission work asked me to give my testimony on the radio in Low German! By the grace of God, I was able to do so, and I knew that was the answer to my prayer on what could I do.

We went to the same area again the next year and I taught English there in their elementary school in the evenings. The students arrived after dark, by horse and buggy! It was an amazing experience; so much more I could share.

We have heard that there was a revival since then; some of the OC men went to a men's retreat and found Jesus! Many left the OC (excommunicated because they studied the Bible on their own), but they have now filled the EMMC church, and the Christian school is almost filled up as well. For this we give thanks. (Read more about this in the Epilogue.)

Back to our life in Neepawa: But this time, my husband's eyes were deteriorating from glaucoma, and we knew it was time for change. So we plowed up our 4 acres of strawberries (Klassen Berry Farm), and turned it into 6, 2-acre lots which are now all sold, as well as the beautiful house Ruben built for me! We moved to Steinbach in 2018 and feel like we've come home! We have met old friends and new ones. We are much closer to Ruben's siblings and to three of our four children. But we miss the daughter we left behind who lives in Brandon. She is not quite as lonely because she just got married to Murray, the Mister Right she has long been waiting for!

Eleven

BISHOP JOHANN LOEPPKY'S MINISTRY BY ABRAM G. JANZEN

H ere are the writings of Abram G. Janzen formerly of Hague, Saskatchewan in regard to our grandfather:

Rev. Loeppky was a Saskatchewan Old Colony Mennonite Altester. A gifted and devoted man, his preaching, counsel, and personable manner were widely appreciated. One pivotal development was his decision not to join the 1920's migration to Mexico. Subsequently, he became the key leader in helping Old Colony churches in Canada to become re-established. However, in 1948 he did lead a migration to Mexico. This did not work out as he had hoped so he soon came back. He died six months later. [This was written on February 12, 2023].

Then in his introduction, he goes on to give more background and further details:

I recall Altester Johann Loeppky from my childhood in the 1920's. He would often stop at our farm in the village of Neuanlage, four miles south of Hague, and come into our house with a smile and a friendly greeting for everyone. My sister Helen had a beautiful voice and my mother had taught her to sing. Even when Helen was only four, Rev. Loeppky would say, "Na Lena, dann sing amol wada." (Now Helen, please sing something again.) Then Helen would sing a song like, "Wo Willst Du Hin Weils Abend ist," #693 in the old German "Gesangbuch". She would sing the whole song and Mr. Loeppky would praise her for it.

Many years later, even after Helen had become a grandmother, when she met Rev. Loeppky, he would say, "Na Lentje, singst noch emma?" (My dear Helen, do you still sing?)

Johann Loeppky was born in the village of Blumenfeld, south of Winkler, Manitoba, on January 21st, 1882. His mother, Maria nee Martens, was a sister to my father's mother Susana nee Martens. This made Rev. Loeppky a first cousin to my father Peter Janzen. That is one reason for his frequent visits to our farm.

Tragically, Johann Loeppky's father died before he was born. (His death was an accident. The horses he was driving got excited for some reason. They took off in different directions and he became tangled in the reins.) Johann Loeppky's mother remarried in 1883. Her new husband was Isaak Dyck. Incidentally, this new couple, Isaak and his wife Maria, had a son, who later became Altester Isaak M. Dyck, the prominent church leader in the Manitoba Colony in Mexico who, near the end of his life, wrote the book "Auswanderung der Reinlander Mennoniten von Kanada nach Mexico". Part of it is printed later on in this writing (with permission from the Delmar Plett Foundation who had it translated into English in 2022 by Robyn Sneath.)

Johann Loeppky grew up in the Dyck household* in Blumenfeld, Manitoba, the same village where my father grew up. (*My Aunt Helen Schmidt has a correction here: Johann Loeppky lived in the Dyck household only until he was six years old. His stepfather took him to the barn where he got a terrible spanking. His mother intervened, took him by the hand and brought him to his maternal grandparents.) [Author's note: It is believed he also stayed with an English family at some point where he apparently learned some English, how to play the fiddle and even how to dance! He moved to Saskatchewan when his grandparents did.]

Early in the 1900's Loeppky moved to what in 1905 would become the province of Saskatchewan. There he married Anna Neudorf and settled in the village of Reinland, just north of Osler. (My father married Helena Guenther in Manitoba. They moved to Saskatchewan in 1905 and settled on an isolated farm but in 1909 they joined the Loeppkys in Reinland and in 1913 they moved to Neuanlage.) In those years, there was no church in Reinland so for worship services the people travelled to Neuanlage, about six miles north. Mr. Loeppky had a strong voice so he was soon asked to be a Vorsaenge. Not long thereafter, in 1909, he was elected to be a minister. That same year, in July, his wife died, leaving him with four young children, two boys and two girls. My mother then took the boys into her care.

In September of 1909, just two months after his first wife died, Rev. Loeppky married Helen Janzen who, despite the Janzen name, is not related to me. Interestingly, the day after the wedding, the bride had to serve meals to a threshing crew, meaning at least fifteen men. My mother and some other ladies went to help her in this formidable task. The new Mrs. Loeppky took on three of Rev. Loeppky's children but the fourth, the oldest son, was adopted permanently by Mrs. Jacob Neufeld who had no children of her own. Rev. Loeppky always kept close contact with this son despite the separation. (*My aunt Helen reports that he tried many times to get him back but was unsuccessful*).

Alongside his family responsibilities, Rev. Loeppky's heart was steadfast in the ministry of the church. He was gifted for this work. He was easy to listen to. I remember one spring when the grass was green and the flowers were coming into bloom, my brother-in-law who worked on our farm, that is, my parents' farm, asked me on Monday morning if I had been to church on Sunday. When I said that I had not, he said, "You should have been there; Rev. Loeppky was preaching." The custom in those days was for ministers to read their sermons without comment but Rev. Loeppky interspersed his sermons with comments in Low German. On this occasion he had spoken about the beauty of God's creation, saying that the singing of the birds, the budding of the trees, and the blooming of the flowers, all showed the creative hand of God and that God loved beauty and that is what God was seeking in our hearts-joy and praise. My brother-in-law was very moved by the way Rev. Loeppky had spoken. He said he had never heard a sermon like that before.

I still recall a sermon, after more than fifty years, when Rev. Loeppky spoke about the crucifixion of Christ. He made it seem so real that I could almost see the Roman soldiers as they went about their gruesome task of hammering those nails into the hands of Jesus. Loeppky had tremendous oratorical power as well as a pleasant personality. In the system of the time, ministers circulated among the churches. When Rev. Loeppky's turn came to speak in a particular church, the services were well attended. Also, he was much in demand at funerals, weddings, and "felaffnessen", meaning engagement celebrations. Of course, as Altester, he performed all the baptisms including those for me and my wife. Rev. Loeppky was also a good horseman. His horses were always well-groomed and cared for."

THE 1920S MIGRATION TO MEXICO

After the First World War ended in 1918, the governments of both Saskatchewan and Manitoba began to force changes in the school system. Until this time the Old Colony Church had had private schools in the German language. Since the war was against Germany, German-speaking people were frowned upon by many Canadians.

The governments now decided that despite the "privilegium" (list of agreements) granted to these Mennonites by the federal government in 1873 which gave them complete **freedom** in the education of their children, some basic changes would be made. These Mennonites would have to start sending their children to government schools where the language of instruction was English and the curriculum was set by the government.

The objections of the Old Colony Mennonites led to several years of difficult negotiations. Mennonite leaders in both provinces pleaded with the governments to continue to allow them to have their own schools. They wrote long letters outlining their concerns. The governments, however, stood firm. Indeed, they imposed fines which parents had to pay for each school-aged child whom they did not send to the government schools. In Saskatchewan, in some areas, the authorities were harsh in the way they enforced the fines. Many parents paid fifteen dollars per month per child, selling cattle and land in order to make the payments. After some years of this, many became impoverished. It was a very difficult time.

When the governments refused to modify their policy, the Mennonites began to look for a different country in which to make their homes. Following "brotherhood" meetings, delegations were sent to various places to inquire both about land and about a "privilegium" (agreement letter) so that they would be able to continue their way of life. Rev. Johann Loeppky was prominent in the delegations to Mexico. Indeed, the Hague-Osler delegation had a crucial part in obtaining the "privilegium" letter signed by Mexican President Alvaro Obregon, on February 25, 1921. Loeppky's name is one of six that appear on it. (See Leonard Sawatsky's, "They Sought a Country", p. 37).

The migration to Mexico was a complex undertaking. Not everything went smoothly. One problem had to do with an effort to sell all the land as one unit. A major land agent wanted to buy the whole of the Hague-Osler reserve, believing that he had enough new people to fill it. The church leaders were pleased with the prospect of being able to sell all the land as a unit. In order to prepare for this, they asked all the landowners to sign over the titles of their land to two men, a Mr. Benjamin G and Rev. Johann P. W. These men would hold the titles in trust and once the sale was completed then each landowner would be given money for his particular pieces of land.

The plan to sell all the land in the reserve as one unit was good as far as it went, but as is often the case with human plans, this one fell apart. The land agents either could not, or would not, carry through. As a result, there was no collective sale. That left the people who had signed over their land titles very uncertain. Most now wanted to get their titles back into their names. But how could they do this? The church leaders said that on this matter the people were on their own. The process proved to be slow and costly, in part because the law required the title search for each piece. My father was one of those involved. It cost him $365.00 to get his titles back, which was a lot of money in those days.

In 1926, when the Hague-Osler group did not move, this land titles question had still not been resolved. As a result, the two men, G. and W., both of whom moved, signed enough blank land transfer papers and left them with Mr. A. H. K., a very trusted man, who served as the Justice of the Peace in the town of Hague. Then when the individual owners had enough money they would go to Mr. K., sign the documents, and get their titles back. There was considerable frustration. My father always said that one reason why he, in these years, decided against moving to Mexico laid in the way the church leaders dealt with this situation. It had revealed certain dynamics to which he did not want to be bound.

Rev. Loeppky, not a wealthy man either, was sympathetic to the plight of the people. Many were getting into serious financial hardship because of the school fines that the government kept pressing. For this reason, and to the extent also because of the land title problem, support for the migration declined. Some people were becoming too poor to move. Rev. Loeppky had compassion on them. When he began to see that a good number would not be moving, he felt they would be like sheep without a shepherd. [*The Altester at the time],* was sympathetic too, though he was quieter about it. However, [Rev. W] was adamant. He saw those not moving as disloyal and rebellious. He would say, "The Gemeinde (church) is moving. People, who are not coming, no longer belong to the Gemeinde. We are not responsible for them." When Rev. Loeppky decided not to move, [this minister] and other ministers as well as some of the prominent members became very critical of them. They said he was betraying the church.

This rift within the "Lehrendienst" had many unfortunate and last-ing effects. The people who decided to stay in Canada liked Rev. Loep-pky but many who held to the decision to move now disliked him. Some of the leaders blamed him for the fact that so many, approximately three-quarters of the Hague-Osler church, stayed. A few who stayed also did not like Loeppky. After the departure of those who did move, some of those who stayed back kept writing letters to Mexico saying negative things about Loeppky. One of the criticisms was that he did not excom-municate people as readily as he should, for example, in relation to the growing use of cars. These things encouraged the ministers in Mexico, Rev. Loeppky's former colleagues, to believe that they were right in their negative judgment of him.

One situation in which the lasting negative effect of this rift was apparent involved one of my uncles. He had been excommunicated around 1915 for voting in a municipal election, more specifically, for refusing to apologize for having done this. He and his family did not live in a village. Their farm, somewhat isolated, was on the banks of the South Saskatchewan River, about four miles east of the village of Blumnenheim. In the 1930s, [a Mr. D] who was also a minister from the General Conference Mennonite Church, was the teacher in the public school near Blumenheim. (The school was called Renfrew). Mr. D was a very loving man and since Blumenheim did not have a church building with regular services, he would sometimes hold services in the school on Sunday evenings. Here my uncle was welcome, so he went, together with his family.

When Mr. D discovered that my uncle was under the ban of excommunication, he wanted to help resolve the problem. My uncle then explained to him that this would be very difficult because he had been excommunicated by the ministers who had moved to Mexico, not by those in Canada. Rev. D then, with my uncle's permission, wrote to the church in Mexico to ask if this ban could be lifted. The reply that he received from [Rev. J.P. W], dated September 10, 1933, of which I still have a copy, is a scathing criticism of Rev. Loeppky. [W] said that the church in Mexico had no spiritual fellowship with Loeppky. He blamed him for causing many other people to become unfaithful to the church. To [Rev. W] and to other leaders in Mexico, the failure to move to Mexico represented unfaithfulness to the church. (Rev. Isaak M. Dyck [Rev. Loeppky's own half-brother] also expressed this view. Fortunately, in the mid-1940s my uncle was able to resolve his matter, thanks to the efforts of a new minister, Rev. [A. W.] My uncle then wrote to Rev. [J. P.W] in Mexico and this time he received a gracious response. My uncle lived for six more years. During this time, he became a much more peaceful person. The ban, lasting about thirty years, had nurtured much anger in him. Once that was lifted, he was a very changed man.

The tensions relating to the migration had one other dimension. In 1921, during the exploratory phase, the Old Colony people from Manitoba and those from the Hague-Osler and the Swift Current areas of Saskatchewan worked as one body. Later, there was a split. According to one report, the Manitoba leaders did not want to work with those from the Hague-Osler area when they discovered that the Hague-Osler people would be bringing less money, meaning that, if they bought land in one block, others might end up having to pay more than their share. Whatever the exact reasons, the rift led the Hague-Osler people to buy land separately, in Durango province, approximately 500 miles south of Chihuahua where the Manitoba and the Swift Current people moved in 1922-24. The main Hague-Osler move took place in 1926.

REV. LOEPPKY'S MINISTRY IN CANADA...
AFTER THE 1920S MIGRATION
Though only about one-quarter of the Old Colony people from the Hague-Osler area moved to Mexico, most of the ministers did. Only two, Rev. Loeppky and Rev. Abram Wall, stayed back, as did Deacon [W.W] These two ministers now had to serve in the churches in Neuanlage, Neuhorst, and Edinburgh. In addition, they had to conduct services in Blumenthal and Blumenheim, in the old German school buildings since these two villages did not have church buildings. The two ministers served on a rotation basis. This meant that no church had services every Sunday. In fact, in Blumenthal and Blumenheim services were held only every third Sunday at best, and sometimes not even that often. I remember my father telling us children on Sunday mornings, to run to the far end of our village (Neuanlage) to see if the shutters on the church windows were open. If they were, then there would be worship services that Sunday. The two ministers carried a heavy load of church work. At the same time, they had to earn a living for their families. Since Rev. Wall was not very healthy, Rev. Loeppky's responsibilities were particularly strenuous. He was always busy. In addition to the work in the Hague-Osler reserve, he was also called to Manitoba and to the Swift Current area by the Old Colony people there who had not joined the migration to Mexico. In both of those places, the majority had moved including all of the ministers, leaving the people who stayed back without any church leadership. If there was a funeral or if a couple wanted to get married, Rev. Loeppky was often called to officiate, though Rev. Jacob Wiens, the Altester who had moved to Mexico, did come back to serve at Baptism and Holy Communion services in 1927 and 1928. In 1929 Rev. Wiens again set out on the trip but he was then called back because his wife fell ill. He never came to Canada

again. However, when he died, on April 14, 1932, the Hague-Osler people held a memorial service for him. Whatever people thought about the migration, they still loved Altester Wiens. After the failure of Altester Wiens' last effort, in 1929, to come and serve the church in the Hague-Osler area, the Old Colony people began to talk about electing an Altester of their own. Also, although a few families moved to Mexico as late as 1934, it had become clear that a large number would not be moving. This made it important to get the church to function properly again. Electing an Altester would be a major step. Since there was no Altester left in Canada, Altester Cornelius Hamm of the Saskatchewan Bergthaler was asked to preside over the election. The people who had remained in the Manitoba and Swift Current areas were invited to participate in the election, though the only two candidates were from the Hague-Osler area, these being Loeppky and Wall who, in fact, were the only Old Colony ministers in Canada at the time. Loeppky was elected Altester with a strong majority.

A few days later, on March 20, 1930, Rev. Cornelius Hamm ordained Rev. Loeppky as the Old Colony Altester. I still remember the ordination service. We children could not attend. My parents said there would not be room. But while the service was in progress, we went to see for ourselves. We found the yard packed with horses and sleighs. Some were parked out on the village street, with the horses tied to fence posts. The fact that it was a Bergthaler Altester who ordained Rev. Loeppky as Old Colony Altester, also led to a policy change: no longer would the Old Colony church excommunicate a member simply for marrying a Bergthaler member. Also, after Loeppky's election as Altester, the church formally adopted the name Old Colony Mennonite Church. Earlier the name was Reinlander Mennonite Church.

Rev. Loeppky, now Altester, soon encouraged the holding of a ministerial election. This resulted in Messr. Isaak Wieler and Johann H. Janzen being elected as ministers. Both had been schoolteachers in the German village schools. Now, with four ministers, worship services were held on a more regular basis in all the locations. However, Rev. Isaak Wieler had some other ideas. Before long, he set out to move to Mexico, only to find that the Mexican border was closed. He and his family then came back but one year later they moved to the Fort Vermillion area in northern Alberta, about one thousand miles away, where a number of Old Colony families had recently settled.

After Rev. Wieler left for Fort Vermillion, the church in the Hague-Osler area again had a ministerial shortage. It was not possible to have services at all the places every Sunday. To deal with this, the church, in 1935, held another ministerial election. This time Messers. Abram J. Loewen, Peter T. Neudorf, and Peter Martens were elected as ministers while Mr. Jacob Giesbrecht was elected to be the deacon. All of these men accepted their calling so now the church was fully staffed and services could be held in all the places of worship on a regular basis again. Rev. Peter Martens lived near Edinburgh, across the South Saskatchewan River from the main settlement. This was convenient since the river had to be crossed by ferry in the summer and over ice in winter. In the fall and in the spring, there were always periods of several weeks when it was not possible to cross the river. During these periods Rev. Martens was responsible for serving the Edinburgh church himself.

In the depression years of the 1930s small groups of Old Colony people from the Hague-Osler area moved to Swan Plain, Sonningdale, and other places, simply to make a living. Naturally, they longed for pastoral visits and church services. Rev. Loeppky travelled endlessly. Also, he continued to go to Swift Current, Saskatchewan area and to Manitoba to serve Old Colony people, meaning those who had not moved to Mexico. However, in 1936 in Manitoba, following various discussions, he helped the people there to function as a church again, meaning that he officiated at ministerial elections and ordained elected individuals. One of the elected individuals, Mr. Jacob Froese, was also elected and ordained as Altester for the Manitoba church. It also relieved Rev. Loeppky of responsibilities there.

In the Swift Current area, the Old Colony church was never re-established after the migration to Mexico. Rev. Loeppky went there a number of times to hold services; also, Old Colony young people from there would come to the Hague-Osler area for catechism classes and baptism. But by 1950 the Old Colony people there had either moved to a settlement that had an Old Colony church or joined the Sommerfelder church in the Swift Current area. Interestingly, Old Colony people there invited the Sommerfelder church to take over some of the church buildings after the main Old Colony group had left for Mexico.

REV. LOEPPKY'S FRIENDLY AND WISE MANNER

Although Altester Loeppky's workload was heavy, he maintained a friendly personal manner. One story comes from a trip to Fort Vermillion, Alberta where he went to baptize people and to officiate at Holy Communion services. In 1939, he went there to also hold ministerial elections. The trip was strenuous. From the town of Peace River, he and several men with him had to take a river boat to Fort Vermillion, a distance of about two hundred and fifty miles. The boat was a freight boat that stopped frequently to load or unload goods. The men with Rev. Loeppky later reported that they had sometimes left him alone on the deck, thinking that he would want to reflect on things by himself, and that when they had been by themselves they had often smoked. Smoking, though frowned upon, was not prohibited and in this context, it helped to chase at least some of the mosquitoes away, since they had been terrible. One time Rev. Loeppky had requested that they blow some of their smoke over him so as to also chase some of the mosquitoes away from him. That the Altester would make such a request had been quite amusing to these men. In a 1941 trip to Fort Vermillion Rev. Loeppky officiated in an election for Altester Rev. Wilhem P. Wiebe who was elected to that office. Rev. Loeppky ordained him. This reduced the need for Rev. Loeppky to make that long trip.

During the 1941 visit to the Fort Vermillion area, Rev. Loeppky's wisdom was evident in another way. There were three young brothers who, with their wives, had moved to that northern community from the Osler area on their own. They were not members of the Old Colony church. For this and perhaps for other reasons, the Colony people tended to avoid them, almost to the point of shunning them. When these men heard that Rev. Loeppky would be conducting a service, they went uninvited. One of them later told me, "We were apprehensive, not knowing whether we would even be allowed into the church. But we knew Rev. Loeppky from our days in Saskatchewan and we wanted some news about our parents who were good friends of the Loeppkys. We stood a distance from the door of the church. People were eyeing us suspiciously but when Mr. Loeppky came into the yard and saw us he came up with a big smile and welcomed us with a warm handshake, saying, "Na jounges, daut freit me ycount hea to seenen." (Well boys, I am glad to see you here). This broke the barrier and many people then came to shake hands with us and bid us welcome."

In another migration, in 1940, a sizable group from Hague-Osler settled in the Burns Lake area in British Columbia. The move was supported by both the Saskatchewan and British Columbia governments. It was a way of dealing with the poverty in Saskatchewan that had resulted from the depression and the drought of the 1930s. For these Old Colony Mennonites, the prospect of settling on the British Columbia frontier seemed like a good solution. But the move meant that Rev. Loeppky now had to travel also to that settlement to serve the people. In one visit to Burns Lake, Rev. Loeppky helped to resolve a particular problem. The custom was that after church the people would come to the place where Rev. Loeppky was staying so as to visit and to ask about friends and relatives back in Saskatchewan. This visit, in 1942, was the time when the Federal government had implemented the Family Allowance program, giving parents five dollars per month for each child under sixteen years of age. Many people in the Old Colony church declined this allowance saying that if the government paid for raising the children, then it would, in case of war, claim that the children had an obligation to render military service. On this occasion, a lady with a loud voice asked Rev. Loeppky, "Is it true that in Saskatchewan some of your church members are accepting this allowance?" In an instant, the room was quiet since this was a controversial issue. All waited for Rev. Loeppky to respond. When he responded calmly saying that yes it was true, the lady burst forth, "And you allow that? It is totally wrong; should you not punish people for this?" (Punishment meant excommunication).

Rev. Loeppky then explained, "Maybe you are right, maybe it is wrong to accept this allowance; however, we as a church have not done our duty. As you well know, in years past it was our custom that people would bring vegetables, dried fruits, smoked meat, grain and other things from our harvest to 'the storehouse of the Lord' (In the Neuanlage church the place above the ceiling was used for storing such things.) Then when people were in need, they would go to our deacon who would then give to them from these goods. However, the people in the church became hard-hearted and disobedient. As a result, there is nothing in our church storehouse. Because of this, our loving God, in His wisdom, has moved our government to collect from those who have in the form of income tax. This, our people pay willingly because if they don't, they will be penalized. The government then gives this income tax money to families. In this way, those who have abundance help those who lack. This brings about a little more equality, as we are taught in the Bible, in 2 Corinthians 8:14-15." After Rev. Loeppky had spoken, everyone was quiet for a while. Then the lady with the questions asked, "Is that how it really works?" "Yes," Rev. Loeppky said. Then the lady said, "If that is so then it makes sense. I think I will apply for it too because we hardly have enough to eat at times." Most of the people nodded in agreement. Before long, most Old Colony folks received the monthly family allowance cheques.

Rev. Loeppky made many visits to places like Burns Lake. He was on the road a lot. I well recall that when he would speak in the Neuanlage church he would report on his most recent visit to some distant settlement. The people appreciated these reports. Many had relatives in various new settlements. In 1945, Rev. Loeppky ordained Rev. Johann Martens as Altester for the Burns Lake group. Now he did not have to travel there as often.

Another story shows Rev. Loeppky's practical approach to things. I had an uncle who lived some distance away. He was rather conservative. One time he and his family came to visit, driving a 1926 Maxwell car. In those days, there were no filling stations. When they wanted to return home my uncle measured the gasoline, pushing a stick into the tank since in those days they did not have gas gauges. He said, "I am not sure that this will take us home. Do you have some gasoline?" "Yes," my father answered. He then asked for three gallons and my father poured in that amount. Then my uncle asked about the price. My father answered it was 25 cents per gallon. "That's fine," my uncle replied, "but since it's Sunday is it all right if I pay you later?" he asked. My father agreed because it was not uncommon for people to avoid using money on Sundays in those days.

In contrast, one winter evening when the snow was blowing, my father saw someone coming onto the yard with a sleigh so he called the boys to go and unhitch the visitor's horses and take them into our barn. The visitor turned out to be Rev. Loeppky but before we could unhitch his horses he told us not to do so, saying, "I have just come from a funeral in Blumenthal and since I go past your place anyway I thought I would pick up that pair of bridles your father and I talked about the other day." My father then told me which bridles they were and I ran into the barn to get them. Then Rev. Loeppky asked about the price. When I told him it was two dollars, he reached into his pocket, paid the money, bade farewell and drove home. When we came into the house my father had an amusing smile on his face. Mother wanted to know what was funny. Father then explained, saying, "This is money and today is Sunday. Altester Loeppky paid for the bridles." "Well, shouldn't he?" Mother asked. "Yes", replied Father, "but in the summer your brother needed gasoline but since it was Sunday he would not pay until I met him some weeks later. Now the Altester himself comes on a Sunday, takes out his wallet and pays for his purchase without giving it a thought." This shows Rev. Loeppky's logical way of thinking.

One other story: Soon after I was married, we had visitors from another province, a young Old Colony minister and his wife. Rev. Loeppky then came over with his buggy to ask the visiting minister to speak in one of the churches on Sunday. We all stood around the buggy talking for a while and later the young minister's wife told my wife, "It was interesting to visit with Rev. Loeppky because he could laugh so freely. We always thought that ministers should not laugh and it is hard to be serious all the time." This is what endeared Rev. Loeppky to many people. He could face life in such a way that it did not always drag him down.

There were other developments in these years that called for Rev. Loeppky's attention, some related to human problems and some to differences of opinion that come up in any community. One major issue was the Second World War and the effort to secure conscientious objector status for the young men. In this, Rev. Loeppky cooperated with leaders from other churches, including the prominent Bishop David Toews from Rosthern. Rev. Loeppky was authorized to sign certificates for young men but he referred some problem cases to Bishop Toews. Also, during these years, the disease of tuberculosis was a real threat. People who had this disease were sent to sanatoriums for several years of treatment. An Abram Dyck, a young Old Colony man, was sent to a sanatorium in Prince Albert, nearly one hundred miles away, for this reason. On at least one occasion, Rev. Loeppky went to visit him and to serve him with Holy Communion.

THE 1948 MIGRATION TO MEXICO

In the second half of the 1940s there was a new interest among Old Colony people in Burns Lake, Sonningdale, and the Hague-Osler district in another migration to Mexico. The Second World War was over but there was fear about another war breaking out and about possible pressures on Mennonite young men if that would happen, since many had entered the armed forces even now. Besides, the economy was not good. At first, Rev. Loeppky was reluctant about the idea of another migration. However, in 1946 a group went to visit relatives in Mexico. The group included Altester Loeppky and his wife who had a daughter and a son there, my brother-in-law, Jacob B. Wiebe, a single man who had a brother there, Abram Friesens from Grunthal who also had a daughter there, and Johann B. Peters from Blumenheim who had other close relatives there.

This visit seems to have been a turning point for Altester Loeppky. When the group came back, he was interested in getting another migration going. One reason, it seemed, was that the common people in Mexico who remembered him from Canada had expressed very strong appreciation of him, perhaps because they were weary of the strictness of some of their leaders in Mexico. Many had said to him, "If you come to Mexico, we will join your group at once." Unlike the ordinary people, however, the leaders in Mexico, both in Chihuahua and in Durango, had refused to acknowledge him as a fellow minister. Indeed, they had been sharply critical of him. His decision, back in the 1920s, not to move was still a big issue. One other factor supporting the idea of another migration was that most of the returning visitors told positive stories about their relatives' economic situation in Mexico. These sounded good since in the Hague-Osler area there had just been several years of bad crops and the memory of the 1930s depression was still very fresh. As a result of these developments, the fire for another migration was kindled.

Around this time a group from the Kleine Gemeinde in Manitoba also indicated interest. They asked to be included in the negotiations, as did a number of Old Colony families from the Winkler, Manitoba area. In the Hague-Osler area, the interest led to a number of meetings. I attended several. This led to more trips to Mexico and eventually to the purchase of a piece of land in the state of Chihuahua. Soon there were auction sales where people sold what they could though, because of the bad economic situation, the sales did not yield much. In the fall of 1948, a train pulled out of Osler taking a large group to their new home. Several train cars were filled with farm machinery. Several families moved by truck. My wife's mother and seven of my wife's brothers and sisters, three of whom were married and had families of their own, were in this migration. (One of my wife's brothers had lived in Mexico in the Durango colony since the migration of 1926.)

Unfortunately, when these 1948 migrants arrived in Mexico there were troubles. Already when they crossed the border one woman, upon seeing the Mexican people, cried out, "I never wanted to come here. Take me back." Her husband had not been able to console her. When the group arrived at their first destination and found only a few old Mexican adobe ranch buildings the dissent increased. Barely five months later two families were back in Canada, disgruntled and much poorer. Their return led many who were still thinking of moving to reconsider. Those who had pushed for the move now became very quiet. In fact, a number started blaming Altester Loeppky for starting the migration idea, even though some of these same people had clearly said, "If you move we will follow."

In December 1949, my wife and I, with five small children, went to visit my wife's mother and her siblings and their families. On the first morning after we arrived, I walked over to Rev. Loeppky's place. It was December 15, 1949. I saw immediately that he was a different man. He was much more burdened and serious. The first thing he asked me was. "Have you come to stay?" I said we had come to see the situation. Then he asked by name about the families who had promised to come. I reported that not one of them had said anything about moving for a long time. He then commented, "I thought so because the letters have stopped coming." Also, he said that people from the older colonies who had wanted to join him had been told they would be excommunicated by their churches, so they had not come. Two families who had come to Los Jagueyes had been excommunicated. As a result, no one else felt free to come and before long these two had returned to their original colony because that was the only way they could resolve their excommunicated state. In the conversation with Rev. Loeppky, I could feel that he had given up his dream for this new settlement. He also said there was no unity among those already there, that the people from Manitoba and those from Burns Lake could not agree.

A few days later he told my brother-in-law, Jacob B. Wiebe, who did the legal work for the settlement that he would be moving back to Canada. This news sent a shock through the settlement. It was a severe blow. My mother-in-law, who with Mrs. Loeppky, were the two oldest women there, felt saddened beyond words. She had not been enthusiastic about the move in the first place but since she was a widow with a son who, in the event of another war, would be of military age, she had agreed. Now she would be alone and the group would remain small and weak at best.

REV. LOEPPKY'S RETURN TO CANADA AND HIS DEATH

Rev. Loeppky's decision to return to Canada also had implications for the Kleine Gemeinde people. He had provided the legal umbrella for them to come into Mexico, being able to do this because his name was on the 1921 "privilegium" letter from the Mexican President. This meant that he had to sign for each family in order for them to get legal permission to live in Mexico. The Kleine Gemeinde had at least twenty families in Manitoba who were still planning to come. How would they now get their papers signed? Two Kleine Gemeinde leaders now came to Rev. Loeppky and asked if he would sign a number of uncompleted forms for them so that after he was gone their people could still enter Mexico. Rev. Loeppky replied, "I am willing to do that but I must have permission from the brethren". He had already set a date for an auction sale to dispose of his possessions so he called a brotherhood meeting for Saturday night because on Sunday morning he would preach his last farewell sermon and on Sunday afternoon he would leave, together with the Aaron Unruhs form Burns Lake who were also returning to Canada. Rev. Loeppky then invited these two Kleine Gemeinde leaders to attend the Saturday evening brotherhood meeting. One was a Mr. Plett, the other a Mr. Reimer. I think both were ministers. I went along to this meeting as a visitor. Rev. Loeppky opened the meeting with a short devotional and then he came to the question of whether the brotherhood would authorize him to sign the papers for the Kleine Gemeinde group so that their families still planning to come from Canada would be able to do so. He said he felt obligated to sign since it had been part of the original agreement of the Old Colony group with the Kleine Gemeinde that he do so. However, he said he felt he needed permission from the brethren. He then asked people to express their views either for or against, but no one spoke up. He asked again, pleading that people express their views either for or against. Still, no one spoke. Then one of the Kleine Gemeinde men asked if they should go outside. Rev. Loeppky said there was no need for that, but they went out anyway. Then Rev. Loeppky tried again but still no voice was heard. He even turned to one of the ministers seated behind him but even he did not speak up. Then Loeppky said, "Brethren, if you do not speak up then the whole thing comes to a standstill and what will happen then?" He begged several more times without success. Finally, I could not stand it any longer so I said, "I am a visitor and I have no say in the matter but it seems to me that if the forms are not signed, then the additional families will not be able to come and then the money that they would bring will not be available to make the upcoming payment on the land and if that payment cannot be made then all the land and the whole investment might be lost because the land for the Old Colony and the Kleine Gemeinde are joined in one contract."

In light of this, I suggested that it seemed better if the forms were signed. I got some dark looks from some people, but Rev. Loeppky was overjoyed. He then asked whether there was support for what this brother had put forward and if there was then they could indicate their agreement by being silent. Again, no one spoke up so after a moment of waiting Rev. Loeppky announced that since all had remained quiet, he would accept this as a unanimous agreement that he should sign the forms. He then closed the meeting, sat down, signed the forms, and gave them to the Kleine Gemeinde representatives. They were very, very relieved. As we left, several brethren avoided me. Their silence in the meeting reflected the negative feelings against Altester Loeppky that his decision to leave had aroused. In contrast, Rev. Loeppky thanked me for helping him out of a difficult situation. The next morning, he preached his farewell sermon, wished the new settlers God's blessing, and said he was very willing to come and serve them at least once per year if they so wished. That afternoon he left for Canada.

About a week before this, Rev. Loeppky had asked me to drive him to the older colonies in the Cuauhtemoc area. He wanted to talk with Rev. Isaak M. Dyck, his half-brother, to see if the break in their relations could be resolved. He also wanted to talk with a brother-in-law of his who had been excommunicated for having a rubber-tired tractor. Rev. Loeppky wanted to encourage him to settle his excommunication even if it meant giving up the tractor. Unfortunately, neither of these men was home. Rev. Loeppky was very disappointed. Still, the trip gave us a chance to talk.

In the morning, on the way to Cuauhtemoc, we passed two Mennonite farmers on horse-drawn wagons hauling grain to town. In the evening, on our way home, we passed them again. They had still not reached town and the horses were clearly exhausted. I then commented that if I was in Mexico, I would be excommunicated since the rule against rubber-tired tractors had the effect of forcing these men to spend three days away from their families when, with a truck, it could all be done in one day. To me, this seemed very wrong. Rev. Loeppky urged me not to talk lightly about the ban of excommunication, but he acknowledged that there was a serious problem and that things would have to change.

Rev. Loeppky returned to Canada and arrived in the Hague-Osler area in February 1950. There the church leaders welcomed him warmly as Altester but some of the brethren were cool toward him. They felt he should not have moved to Mexico in the first place, that the whole endeavour had been unwise. The initial arousal of interest in the move and the commitment to it on the part of many people and then, later, their decision not to move seemed like a betrayal of those who had moved. Some understandings among people were broken at this time, never to be fully healed. In Mexico, the Old Colony settlement at Los Jagueyes did not survive.

After Rev. Loeppky left, some others also left. Several families joined the Somerfelder. Others, including a number of my in-laws, eventually moved to the Durango colony, joining people who had moved there from the Hague-Osler area in 1926. However, since these "latecomers" had stayed back in Canada in 1926, it seemed as if they were never fully accepted in Durango. By 1953 the last of the Old Colony people were gone from Los Jagueyes.

After Rev. Loeppky's return to Canada, he lived only another six months. During this time, he conducted a "brotherhood" meeting where it was decided that the church would start using the numerical melody for singing. It was called the "solen Wiese" which moved faster than the "Alte Wiese" which the younger generation did not seem to grasp anymore. However, the church would continue to use the same songbook (Gesangbuch). Rev. Loeppky also presided over the election of two more ministers but before he could ordain them, he became ill and died. His death came from an unusual accident. While eating in a restaurant in Saskatoon, something caught in his throat. He was immediately taken to the City Hospital but seemingly the staff there was unable to help him. On August 20, 1950, at the age of 68 and after only a short stay in the hospital, he died. During that stay, many people came to see him. The nurses expressed surprise, asking. "What kind of man is this that so many people want to see him?" They wheeled his bed into the hall so that more people could at least give him a greeting.

The funeral for Rev. Loeppky, held in the Neuhorst church, was conducted by Altester Jacob Froese from Manitoba. The church was packed and hundreds of people stood outside. For over 40 years, Rev. Loeppky had served as a minister and for twenty of these as Altester. During his ministry, he had preached 2103 sermons, baptized 797 people, and officiated at 198 weddings and 549 funerals. (Leonard Doell, in "Old Colony Mennonites in Canada 1875-2000", ed. by Delbert Plett, p. 143). He was known and loved by many people.

As I reflect on Rev. Loeppky's life, it is clear that he had a key role in helping the Old Colony church in Canada to survive after the 1920s migration to Mexico. What would have happened if Rev. Loeppky had joined in that migration? Perhaps a few more would then also have moved but most would still have stayed back, even if there were no ministers here, no shepherds as it were. Some of these people might have found their way to other churches but some might have drifted into the larger society, never to find a church home again.

It is not too much to say, that Rev. Loeppky was the primary leader who helped Old Colony people in Canada to be a church again after the 1920's migration, thanks primarily to his preaching, but in Manitoba, the Old Colony church ceased to function for over a decade until he helped to get it going again. Years later, the Manitoba church, led by an Altester Penner who had succeeded Altester Froese, had a key role in getting the Old Colony church in Ontario started. Both the Ontario and the Manitoba churches have done an enormous amount to provide church homes for Old Colony people returning from Mexico in recent decades. Rev. Leoppky was the key also, to getting the church at Fort Vermillion, Alberta, going, as well as the one in Burns Lake, B.C. (though the latter closed some decades later.) Also, there is no doubt that his extensive preaching and his wise counsel in many areas planted seeds that have born good fruit in the lives of people though only God can count it.

Alongside these positive assessments, there are questions, particularly about the 1948 migration. Why, really, did Rev. Loeppky decide to lead a migration at this time? Some people speculated that his interest may have become aroused in the 1946 trip to Mexico by the fact that a good number of the people from the 1920s settlements there had come to him and told him that if he established a new settlement in Mexico, they would come and join his. Whether this was a large motivating factor we cannot know. Aside from the question of what motivated him to lead that migration, people wondered, how could he give up on the effort after only fifteen months; and even if it was not working out the way he had hoped, how could he abandon people who had trusted him? Certainly, a good number of people from that migration who stayed in Mexico have had a hard life. Some have suffered severe poverty. The situation of some of my in-laws and their children and grandchildren was genuinely difficult.

Despite the hardship, there is a positive aspect of that migration. It enabled the Kleine Gemeinde to become established in Mexico. Rev. Loeppky's involvement made that possible. Some decades later they helped Old Colony leaders in very substantial ways, particularly in colonies where the Old Colony leaders moved away rather than give in to the pressure for change. The Kleine Gemeinde had better schools. They allowed rubber-tired tractors and trucks. They had more activities for young people and their Christian teaching attracted many. Maybe the hand of God was behind this.

Rev. Loeppky was human. At a few points, it appears, he did not judge wisely. But on the whole, he was a truly outstanding servant of our Lord and his church. The Bible, in Hebrews 13:7 says, "Remember your leaders, those who spoke to you the Word of God..."

May this story help us to do that in honour of this remarkable man, Rev. Johann M. Loeppky."

This marks the end of this narrative by Abram G. Janzen, who had some editorial assistance from his son William Janzen of Ottawa. I contacted William to get permission to use this narrative as it so aptly describes our grandfather's life and work. This he gave to me generously. Our family deeply appreciates this. So thank you William for allowing us to share the writings of your father Abram. I was also given permission to change things if needed; I left out some names as I felt led but otherwise, it is all his original words.

Here is the journal my grandfather wrote on his trip to Mexico. Some sentences may lose something in the translation as the saying goes, as this has been translated from the original German.

Twelve

AELTESTER JOHANN LOEPPKY'S JOURNAL
ON A TRIP TO MEXICO - 1921

Bishop Loeppky and his wife Helen Janzen.

This journal was written by Johann Loeppky, Aeltester of the Old Colony Mennonite Church in Saskatchewan, north of Saskatoon, on his trip to Mexico, in which he investigated settlement possibilities for his church:

On January 19, 1921, Administrator Benjamin Goertzen and I went on a trip to Mexico. Yes, while times are changing so also has come the time of not having freedom in our own schools. So we have agreed, three congregations, one from Manitoba, one from Swift Current (southern

Saskatchewan), and we from the old west, to search for land where we can again have our freedom of schools and such. The three congregations pushed for a single congregation immigration because of the lack of school freedom. All we have seen and heard makes us fear for our beloved young people, who are now very wild, unruly, unrestrained and unbridled in their way of life, and who also don't honour their parents or the church. They don't want to listen, but live free and are impudent in this world. Therefore, the above three congregations have often had brotherhood meetings to discuss what can or could be done.

Many trips have been made to the Government to ask them to give us, through grace, the freedoms which were offered to our forefathers in 1873 before they emigrated from Russia and which were offered to them in Canada again. Could we again have these freedoms in our churches and schools? Their answer was, "You can have your freedom of the church, but the schools were the responsibility of each provincial government itself, and the provinces have rules of their own against which the Dominion Government does not interfere." When we spoke to the provincial government, they told us because of all the nationalities, they had to put English into the schools.

So up until now we three congregations have not been able to teach our way, because the school rules are compulsory. All children from 7 to 15 are to attend public school for ten months of the year. However, they offered us if we would teach some English in our German school, even if only one hour a day, they would let us have our old ways. Yet, we feared this compromise. We gathered many times, had meetings and decided to immigrate to a different country, as we could no longer have our way of teaching with God's word. (Read Mark 10:23).

As mentioned before, many travels and trips were made, to search for freedom of schools, etc. They travelled to South America and the west side of Mexico, but always returned with unsatisfactory results. Mexico, however, did not leave us hopeless so we didn't give up on this possibility. Again and again, meetings were held, with considerations, prayers and begging for guidance, and then again, we started on our huge project. The administrator Mr. B. Goertzen and I from the old west, David Rempel from Swift Current, and Minister Julius Loewen,

Uncle Klaas Heide, and Cornelius Rempel from Manitoba, finally all agreed to go to Mexico, in hopes of getting our freedoms.

However, it was not a simple task or trip we were undertaking, such as going sightseeing from one place to another. I, especially, feel inexperienced and humbled to go and appear before the government and ask for freedom for our way of life. We hoped and prayed that God would be with us on our trip on this serious task to help us conquer all our fears and trials. On January 19, 1921, we left Osler, in hopes of returning, and praying that God would be with us on our journey. My wife and I prayed together and asked our daughters to pray also on the morning of our departure. I also prayed in weakness to ask forgiveness of all my sins through his grace, also praying for a safe return to my family and congregation.

When all our tears that we shed for thee, but by thee are written in heaven, that I through grace can reach where all yours are, who have come through great troubles.

Who have washed their clothes and have made their clothes bright in the blood of the Lamb, O Lord, may I now and forever pray, erase through Jesus' blood, and through grace fare good with me. In this world, I can earn nothing, even if I have made a trip. I am still only dust and ashes, yes, a sinful person. Through the promise of thy dear Son, namely, that nobody shall be lost but rather gathered by him, I dare to pray: Lord through grace, go not with me in judgement and cast me not from thee, then my emotions of fear will break.

As has been mentioned before, we left on January 19th from Osler for Saskatoon. As our tickets had been bought from here to go to Winnipeg, we left at 12:12 pm, via C.P.R. with good weather and health for both families. The long train started slowly and we sat quietly, sad, among all these strange people. In our passenger car, all was quiet and peaceful, in hopes that we would again return to the town of our departure. The train gained speed as we went past one town after another.

The next morning on January 20th at 7:00 a.m. we arrived in Winnipeg. We found accommodations to stay until our groups from Manitoba and Swift Current arrived. There were no arrivals from Swift Current on the next train although telegram arrangements had been made prior to leaving. We went back to our hotel to wait for the Gretna, Manitoba train. In the meantime, our deacon became ill with pains in his leg, an injury from back home. Mr. Goertzen's condition grew worse. He was unable to walk around town, spending most of his time in bed. In this position, I thought to myself, I can't stay in this town any longer. When the train from Manitoba was supposed to arrive, I went alone to meet my group. At home, I had sent word with Minister Peter Harms (who was then visiting out west), to my brother Minister Isaak Dyck, that I would very much like to see him before we left for Mexico. Yes, when the train came, my brother Isaak Dyck and deacon Isbrand Friesen (from the Manitoba colony) were there to see if we had really come. How glad I was to see these two men, amongst all these strange people. We embraced dearly and shook hands. I thanked them heartily for coming and asked whether their delegates had not received the earlier mentioned telegraph of our arrival in Winnipeg. They said that they had their gathering on Thursday in Reinland and had not received any word. They came because of the message I had sent with Minister Peter Harms to my brother Isaak Dyck.

They wanted to take us with them to their colony. I told them of the sick deacon, Mr. Goertzen, who was still in the hotel room. In telling of his sickness, time passed quickly, and we agreed to go with these two men to their colony. The deacon was a little better on Thursday morning, after a somewhat better night, so we left Winnipeg for the colony in the morning.

On Friday we again went to Winnipeg and continued our trip with a few more people from Swift Current. A widow, by the name of Mrs. Abram Kornelson (Waiseman), told us of many experiences in her lifetime. She was sick with cancer and was on her way to see a doctor in Rochester, but had just brought her family to stay with relatives in the colony. This sick widow told us of many hardships she had endured, of her suffering, and how she had earnestly prayed to God to embrace her, and through grace help her. It was a great help, on our important journey, to remember how much she had endured, and she gave us faith and hope. Many tears were shed by her in a short time on the train. God is a precious friend who so gladly wants tears, at least those that come from a true believer, from one who hungers and longs for his Grace. Hopefully, he will enter her name in the everlasting testament, and for all her sorrows and suffering through grace be rewarded.

In the scriptures, flowing tears are like sheaves. Tears show that a person's heart has softened and that the Lord plans to enter into one's heart, and does so in a person following the holy trail by his Son. In this manner is a person born again through the holy seed, and one becomes a much better person after enduring sadness and hardships. Yes, my beloved, after repentance, everything is important. One is spiritually raised from the dead and works to serve the living God. As Jesus said, "The words I speak are Spirit and Life."

When we arrived in the colony, we went to Uncle Isbrand Friesen's for dinner and then on to Gnadental to see my brother Abe Dyck, who took us to my home place where I was born on January 29, 1882. We arrived at my parents' place towards the evening and I stayed the night and had a long talk. The next day my relatives came to see me and with tears in their eyes wished me God's blessing and God's help to bring me back safely. Many a song we sang together. When one can once again enter into one's parent's home, to see where one's cradle once stood, to be with parents and relatives, one becomes childish. Your heart softens; there's so much love and honour, then one gets the feeling to say, "Lord, I am not worthy for all the trust and faith you have bestowed on me, a humble servant." Oh, if only I could one day be saved when I die, also likewise for my parents and relatives, that we may meet someday in that heavenly home, and singing of the righteousness, who have come through great toils and who have washed their clothes brightly in the blood of the Lord. Oh, what joy that would be, but my beloved, I am still too much a sinful person. Oh Lord, I must say, let grace go before righteousness, because I have no power in me to overcome, as I am only a reed swaying in the wind. By grace, weak as I am, help me, through thy great mercy.

The next day was Sunday, and we went to church, to the old prayer house in Reinland, where a huge congregation had gathered to hear us. I had chosen for my text Rev. 2: 1-5. When I think back to that time, how many brothers wished me God's nearness, and closeness on such a trying trip, I must say, may God bless you and I hope he has heard your earnest prayers. Often the words of David in Psalm 133 have entered my mind, "How wonderful and pleasant it is when brothers live together in harmony." Yes, the brother love has kept us together.

From church, I went along with my brother-in-law, Abram Friesen to Schoenwiese for dinner, and visited my sister who heartily welcomed me. After visiting there, I went to Minister Jacob Loewen from Blumengard to see Klaas Heide. My brother Isaak Dyck also came in the afternoon, and the time went by fast. Our Deacon came over in the evening, having visited his in-laws in the village. I soon saw that he wasn't feeling better, walking with a limp as he came into the room, and so we first talked about his illness and then discussed other subjects. Mr. Goertzen was quiet, didn't talk much, and was very patient, but helpful with advice. Aeltester Johann Friesen came over also and gave us many comforting words for our trip. He gave me God's blessing and bade me farewell. He was in full hope that we would not come back unfruitful. Brother Isaak Dyck and I stayed the night at the Heide's and this was the first time in our lives that my brother and I stayed together and we talked for a long time. Our hearts were both so bound together, just like David and Jonathan's. The night wasn't long and morning soon came with limited time left.

It was Monday morning and we prepared to continue on our trip. Time passed quickly, and soon it was time to say farewell to my brother. Mrs. Heide prepared a meal to take with us. After breakfast, our transportation of horse and buggy, waited for us, as their son was supposed to take us to Gretna. In hopes of meeting again, our last goodbyes were said. The Lord will make it possible since this is all done for the foundation of our faith. We left Heide's at 11 a.m., and after about two miles, we found out that Uncle Klaas Heide had left his passport at home, so we turned around and went back quickly, got the passport and soon we were on our way again. It wasn't long before we arrived in Gretna, and boarded the train, which was supposed to take us to Winnipeg. In Rosenfeld, Uncle David Rempel, who was from Swift Current, boarded. He had also been in the colony visiting his in-laws in Rosenfeld, that is, if I'm not mistaken.

So we were now all together, heading for the big city of Winnipeg. In Winnipeg, we met Uncle Johann Wiebe from Herbert, Saskatchewan, who welcomed us heartily and wanted to give us a helping hand on our long journey. Once in Winnipeg we quickly went to apply for our passports. It was soon nighttime and so we found a place to rest.

Tuesday morning came and we had to return to pick up our passports. At the American Consul, things were not easy, but finally after being deeply questioned, our papers were ready. On January 25, at 4:45 p.m., we left Winnipeg, arriving the morning of the 26th at 8:30 a.m. in St. Paul, Minnesota. Two train officers met us, who must have received word from Uncle Johann Wiebe that he would be travelling with us. The two took us to their huge office where we could stay until the train left for Kansas City.

Here in St. Paul our dear Deacon became concerned about his leg, which was not getting any better. He talked about returning home, which gave me some concern because I didn't want to be the only one from our congregation. The trip was too important. We encouraged him to travel one more day to Kansas City, with the hopes that he would feel better then. Uncle Johann Wiebe bought a cane for him and he agreed to continue travelling. We left the next day at 2:55 p.m. On the train, Uncle Heide was greatly concerned about Mr. Goertzen's leg. He doctored it by massaging it and washed it with medicine. When I think of these men, with their fatherly concern they helped out so Mr. Goertzen could stay with us. They showed their love as best they could, but where was our returned love?

We travelled all night and arrived in Kansas City, Kansas at 7:00 a.m. Our Deacon felt much better, having slept somewhat. His leg didn't hurt as much now. We were all in better spirits and we again felt our prayers were answered. Praise the Lord and forget not all the good He has done for thee. He, who forgives all our sins, heals all our wounds, both in the flesh and in the soul. He has saved our lives through redemption and through Grace he has given us health, Psalm 103. The Deacon really enjoyed his breakfast with us the next morning. We left again on the train at 9:25 a.m. Slowly the train started, travelling southwest. We were now far from home, and our thoughts were often with the loved ones we had left behind. Our trip continued, closer and closer to Mexico.

We travelled all day, without many stops, and arrived at the border city, El Paso, Texas, on January 29 at 1:05 p.m. I was amazed to see such a big city so far south. I had also been amazed at the huge mountains we had seen in Texas. The earth was very red and nothing grew but cacti. It was strange for us from the cold north to see the warm south. The cattle were so thin and wandered among the cacti. The weather was beautiful and then we met with snow. It got colder; we even saw snow fences. We were higher than sea level, but before we reached El Paso, the snow was all gone, and it was warm again. Arriving in El Paso, we looked for quarters to stay in so we could rest after our long trip. Evening came shortly, and our thoughts again wandered over hills and mountains, as though on the wings of an eagle, to our beloved ones at home, including our dear congregation. In fellowship, we all sang, prayed and praised Him who had so graciously helped us thus far. To him be honour and praise from now until eternity. When we went to bed the deacon was feeling much better.

It was 5 degrees Fahrenheit on the morning of January 29th. After we went for breakfast, we wanted to get our passports stamped. Arriving at the Mexican Consul, we saw a long line of people. We didn't know what to do, because we could not enter the Consul. If we stayed, we would have to join the line; instead, we agreed to go back to our quarters. Once there, we talked about many things, including the papers we had brought with us to present to the Mexican Government. It was agreed to send a copy of our requested privileges from El Paso to Mexico City so that they could there read and approve our requests, as we wanted to travel on to the west coast of Mexico to look at land. Uncle Johann Wiebe studied the papers to make sure there were no mistakes. His English was better than his German. Some papers had been written in English at home. Mr. Wiebe said that some wording was not properly translated and the meaning was different from what was intended. He thought it would be wiser to hand them our papers in English so they could translate them into Spanish. We had copies made and sent one to the Mexican Government.

When we were almost finished with our papers, the Deacon, Mr. Wiebe, and I saw Mr. Rempel and the others coming for us. They had been looking for us because the line-up was gone and now it was time to go to the Consul. It was only a short while, and we were finished. Our plans were to leave today, but Mr. Wiebe had sent a telegram to Mexico City, to a man named Arthur J. Bronof. Mr. Bronof sent another man named Daniel Solis Lopez, to give us free tickets or make arrangements for the same at the border. Mr. Lopez arrived, greeted us heartily, and was ready to take us to Mexico City. Back home, however, we had planned to go to see the land named Culiacan, on Mexico's west coast. By now it was evening, so we all went to bed.

January 31, 1921, at 1 p.m. the train was supposed to leave for Tuscon, Arizona. It was a very long day. We went into the park and saw many animals we had never seen before, at least not by my inexperienced eyes. We also saw a huge camp of soldiers on the border. We asked whether the Mexicans were such a dangerous group of people. We were told, "No, but the United States fears Japan will invade through Mexico". That evening, ready for departure, we were told the train was overcrowded and it would be best to wait until the next morning. More patience. To us, it seemed like a long wait, but on such a long trip you encounter many things, and so once again we went to bed.

February 1, 1921. Today at 1:20 p.m. we again boarded the train. We travelled all day and through God's help arrived in Tucson at 6:00 p.m. The summer weather was beautiful. We have now travelled some 312 miles on this trip, through many different kinds of land, hills and valleys, and seen many cacti. Once again a place to sleep and rest was sought.

February 2, 1921: Today, we went with two automobiles to a border city named Nogales. Mr. Enlaf, a land agent, met us in Tucson and wanted to trade or sell us land in Culiacan. He gave us free tickets on the Southern P.C. Railroad. This railroad goes through Mexico to Rinz where we planned to go later. On our trip to Nogales, we saw modern irrigation, and huge fields of rubber plants, which I had never seen before. We saw some Mennonite farmers but spoke to none. Arriving in

Nogales we went through customs again to get our passports stamped. It was time again to go to our hotel.

February 3, At 7:00 a.m. we again boarded the train and travelled south. We saw orange gardens and many different kinds of fruit trees. The people seemed strange, for as soon as the train came to a stop, there were people on both sides selling food and other things, some of them making themselves loudly heard. The rich and the beggars are all mixed. The pigs are around also and wait for any bit of food which may drop by the wayside. These pigs seemed very skinny, which we were not used to seeing back home. We travelled until 6:30 p.m. and arrived safely in the city of Guaymas. Here we saw a bit of the ocean and our hotel was only a few steps away from the water. A wondrous place for a city, but in the world, there are also many other wondrous or miraculous places. We arrived at our destination in the evening and stayed overnight. We had a restful night in Mexico.

We woke up early and prepared to travel on. Upon awakening, Uncle Johann Wiebe noticed his mattress was splattered with blood. He showed us and we were shocked and astonished. We could not come to any other conclusion other than a murder had taken place there a while back. On the walls and doors were bayonet holes. Yes, we were now in Mexico and this was no news to these people. Upon dressing, I noticed my socks and shoes were damp, presumably caused by the humidity. After breakfast, we were back on the train. There were many people travelling south, and at one time the train circled around a small body of water. The people were very polite and did their best for us. Some of them wanted to know why we were here and where we were going. In one town, a vehicle came near the window of the train and two armed men boarded. A man in the vehicle outside handed bags of gold to the men on the train, one after another, throwing them under the seat, and there were so many that they ran out of room and had to use the aisle as well. After all was loaded, these two fine men sat down quite comfortably in front of us and kept watch over their gold. Before too long, both men fell asleep. People on the train, stepped on the gold when walking through the aisle, but all remained in good order. To our amazement, it looked so plain and matter-of-fact. We travelled all day and night, and before dusk saw some land that we liked. It had some bushes and good soil.

We arrived in the big city of Culiacan at 5:00 a.m. We took a taxi to a hotel and were warmly greeted. We soon found a place to eat breakfast. It was now <u>February 5</u>, and Mr. Enlaf rented a big truck and together we went looking at the land. In the forest, we saw huge cacti. Our uncles said that here we wouldn't be able to drive with horse and wagon. The bushes and trees were dense and almost impossible to walk through. On the ground were many kinds of prickly thorns that poked into our shoes. The soil was good, mostly black loam. After travelling further, we saw some settlers who had already cleared quite a lot of land. In the villages, we saw different kinds of trees and even some flowering trees.

Finally, we came to a much-modernized sugar factory, which operated all year around. Here sugar and syrup were processed in great quantities. Upon observing these great works, I thought to myself that Mexico is far more advanced than Canada because those great sugar cane plantations are a wonder to see. My eyes couldn't see enough of this as Solomon says in Proverbs 27:20, "The eyes never tire of seeing." On one side of the road, sugar cane plantations stretched out as far as the eye could see, and on the other side, banana plantations did likewise. It is amazing to see that the earth is so well equipped to live on and grow things on, (Isaiah 45:18). It bends a young inexperienced person like me, down to the dust, that the works of the Lord are so great and his wonders so many, too many to count. For He lets all different kinds of trees grow to provide food and beauty to behold. Genesis 2:9-10. Out of the earth, he lets water flow to irrigate the garden. This is evident here, for the water comes from the east, out of the hills, in a wide stream that passes on the outskirts of Culiacan, and through the huge expanses used for plantation irrigation, into the ocean. There is continuous warm weather here; summer and winter are no different. From one field to the next it is always growing season. Banana trees require one year to produce and when almost ready, a new shoot appears at the bottom, and after a year the first one dies. Leaves grow three, four or more together. They grow seven feet long and about one-and-a-half feet wide, and they grow only on top. It is wonderful to see. I went and stood under one tree and told my companions, if it rained, I wouldn't get wet. On the top, under leaves, hung many bundles of bananas. The trees are ten to twelve feet tall and higher. We then went to the sugar and syrup factory, where all the activities were shown and explained to us, but they are impossible to describe. With wonder, we saw the ground in Mexico. The various soils we have seen are no comparison to the soil in Culiacan.

We returned to the city via a different road. The road we travelled was a very good, two-lane road. We saw more open land, both settled and under irrigation. Towards evening we arrived back in the city, tired and hungry, so we found a place to eat. After retiring for the night, we discussed our day and the many wonderful things we had seen. The land, bushes, and huge trees, although mostly thorny, were discussed. How did we feel about all of this, and also would our congregations back home approve? Quietness filled our room, especially for Mr. Goertzen and me, for this wasn't the land we wanted to trade our Saskatchewan land for. To tell the truth, we were not satisfied even though the soil was good. We didn't see how our poor people could clear a few acres of the heavy brush, in order to plant a garden. Our people knew nothing about clearing brush and forest, especially after living on the open prairies. Uncle Klaas Heide said that if we wanted this land, he would look elsewhere for land for his congregation because this land had not left a good impression on him either. They wanted to stay close to us, as did the others. We surrendered our thoughts to Him who rules, and sometimes things go differently than we planned. In the evening we wrote to our beloved families and congregations. I slept little that night, as my mind was filled with important issues.

Today is Sunday, February 6. We awoke healthy and praised Him who had watched over us, thanking Him eternally. Sunday is not important to the worldly city. The people were happy and amused and took their disregard for Sunday in stride. We soon noticed they were preparing for holidays on Monday and Tuesday. Parties are a wild urge for worldly people. I thought of the words from Genesis chapter 6 where it talks about God needing to destroy the earth because of how man had corrupted it. They sang and danced until late last night. However, they never bothered us and were always very polite to us. We went to see the huge irrigation canal. It looked very expensive and seemed to involve very hard work.

The next day, Monday, the weather was twelve degrees. It was a wonderful, calm, quiet, warm day. Once again, we went to look at land on the east side of the city. We saw beautiful gardens, pineapples, many different kinds of gardens, and lots of brush and trees. On a small ranch, we saw a well that was twenty-one-and-a-half feet deep, with lots of good water, and beautiful trees. Where branches were cut off these trees, a milky substance ran out. This substance was used to make wax. We also saw redwood trees. The wood is so hard, it is almost impossible to cut. The trees were so different from ours in the North. We also saw a leather factory, where people were working very hard. The owner spoke English well and the workmen were Mexican. Back in the city, we wished to leave, because the wild life of the people there was getting to us. The evening came and we went to bed preparing to get up early the next day.

On February 8 at 6:00 a.m., we left Culiacan on a long train, arriving in Mazatlan at 2:30 p.m. near the big ocean. From Culiacan to Mazatlan was lots of brush and tall trees. It was a nice area and mostly settled. We rested here, as the train had been very crowded. The day came to an end, in this rather peaceful town.

The next morning, on February 9, we awoke refreshed and healthy and praised and thanked the Lord for protecting us in this big city. We all went to the big ocean and saw many ships, both big and small, and even a ship with sails that was preparing to leave. It didn't take long and before we came near, the sail was put up and the anchor loaded, and it started to sail away. At first, it went on a half wind, but it didn't take long and we could only see the white sails which was something my eyes were seeing for the first time. We watched many other ships coming into the harbour that were loading and unloading. Some ships quite a distance away were loaded with smaller boats. We could hear the roar of the ocean while standing on the shore. While we were standing and watching the ocean and hearing the sounds, I thought of how other delegates had twice travelled on the huge ocean, to look at land in South America, but found none, all for our faith and beliefs. "Oh," I thought, "these men did much for their congregation, for it was a dangerous trip. As the scripture says, they who travel on the ocean speak of the dangers of it." Looking at a ship on the ocean, it looks but like a feather swaying to and fro. We walked along the ocean's shore and saw God's wonders. We also saw what people had accomplished, the good roads and in the hills that only held water and rock, people have worked so hard to build a very modern road.

Finally, we climbed onto a large hill. There stood a huge wireless station, Funtenstation. Close to the station stood a high tower one-hundred and-forty-nine feet high. It was in operation. We then went down the hill towards town, and a light rain fell. We went back to our quarters, but Uncle Johann Wiebe went downtown. Because of the rain, he went into a private home and soon noticed his money pouch missing. Shocked he returned and told us. He wanted to report it to the police, so Daniel Solis Lopez went with him. Shortly, he returned with the police, and we were to identify him, by saying that we knew Mr. Johann Wiebe and all was in order. In the meantime, they caught the thief, and Mr. Wiebe got his wallet back, however, ten dollars was missing from the twenty-five dollars he had lost. This happens in Mexico and I will talk more about this later.

We had to stay another night in this town because of the train schedule. We got up early on February 10th and left again by train travelling south. Again, it was a warm day. This train had eight passenger cars and many freight cars. It was the southern train that travelled on Mexico's west side from Mogales to Ruis. As far as this railway goes, we can use USA dollars, because the train belongs to the United States. We arrived safely at 9:00 p.m. in Ruis. We had travelled close to the ocean in some places, with water on either side and farther back through the hills and forests we met small rivers that had no bridges. Down under it was cemented and we got quite a jolt, but this was nothing new in Mexico. Arriving in the evening we had to find quarters, but the hotels were terrible, with small cafes and open on one side. After supper, a place had to be found to sleep. Some of us slept on a wagon and some of us slept in the café. They brought us some beds and bedding and we made the best of it.

The next morning, we again went out to look for some land, and soon came to a city called Tudspoon. One hundred and thirty thousand acres of land was close by. It was cleared and had a few huge trees and some seeded grass. This is <u>February 11,</u> it is eighty-nine degrees Fahrenheit, and fairly hot. Uncle Cornelius Rempel was getting sick. He got out and rested, the Mexican got upset for he wanted to get us to the train station as planned. I showed him my watch and using sign language asked him when the train was leaving. He indicated at 12 p.m. So I told him, "Let's hurry." The Mexican pointed to Mr. Rempel, who was again sitting down, and shook his head. I told our group that we must hurry or else we would miss the train, for we had been told that our departure was at noon. Uncle Klaas Heide said he would take Uncle Cornelius Rempel on his mule in front of him and would help him. Uncle Cornelius Rempel said he could go no further. Uncle Klaas Heide told him even if we couldn't go further, we must still go on, and he would stay to help him.

Our mules were very smart, knowing that we were not good riders, so they were very lazy. Because we travelled so slowly, Solis and the Mexican decided to send a telegram to the train station, asking them to wait until we came. Our guide told us approximately where to ride, and guided us around a mountain through lots of stones, going steeply upwards, and sometimes through deep ruts, so deep that our luggage hit hard against the stones and broke. When we reached the top, our mules were wet. It had been very hard for them. The guide spurred his mule and left us, and we saw how mules can run when they have to, for the telegram had to be delivered fast.

Slowly we travelled without our guide, but we couldn't be slow. Then we saw the mountain where at the bottom lay the town where we were to catch our train. We couldn't see our guide for he was far ahead of us, and the city came closer, or rather, we came closer to the city. We looked forward to leaving our mules. Both men and beasts were tired. We came closer and closer to the city and finally, we saw it. How joyful we all were. The words of a poet entered the mind of this humble servant (myself), and I recalled, "Ye hills and valleys help me to sing, my Jesus to Him be praise, that through so many humble days

I so far have been protected. Have a good night; it is high time for me to leave the past."

As we neared the city it was too bad we didn't stay together. We rode two by two together. As we entered the city on very narrow streets, we got lost. Two others had gone ahead of us. When my partner and I came to a big house, we saw the grey donkey the telegram carrier had ridden in on, but no one was on it. We dismounted and very soon there were helpful people, wanting to feed our mules, and suddenly the guide appeared and told us to hurry to the train station. It meant, getting back on our donkeys, and with our guide giving us directions in a big hurry. He went back to find our other members. We didn't really know where to go, for we couldn't see the city. Then, south of us, we saw a small train moving back and forth behind a house. We thought this must be the station. But where were our partners? The Mexican, our guide, and Solis came from another direction. All the uncles except two were here now. They had taken a wrong road. I stood beside the train, which was now ready to leave, and I could see the others coming. They slowly came down the same road we had come as if they were not sure which road to take. I whistled and waved my cap and told the others. We were all glad, and Solis was preparing our free tickets, but our partners had not arrived. I again went outside and stood beside the people, whistled and waved my cap, until they saw me and hurried.

The baggage was quickly unstrapped from the donkeys, and we boarded and had our luggage handed to us through the train windows. We departed at twelve noon. And so through God's help, we had come through the huge mountains. His ways we cannot grasp. We were often on the edges of deep cliffs and had our donkeys made a mistake, we would have fallen into the deep down yonder. But our donkeys were used to climbing, but to us, it seemed impossible. Often I turned my head the other way. God's grace kept us from all harm. To Him we give praise and thanks until all eternity. In heaven, we want to forever sing hallelujah, but in this troublesome world we are among the heavily burdened pilgrims, and we are often troubled by not knowing if we'll be able to climb the mountains in life. We have to continue climbing, even though the mountains are high, mount Zion from where all help comes is much higher.

How often I have recalled those times when we travelled together, I especially thought of Uncle Cornelius Rempel who often took a rest, quiet and contented, when the rest of us were more restless. Yes, my beloved pilgrims, all of you who will hear and read this, let us go hand in hand so that we will not fall. For the precipices are steep and should we fall, we cannot come to that city, we so often long for. We will surely reach it if we keep on climbing, for there up high shines the crown that Jesus will hand to us when he says, "I am the Way, the Light, the Door through me you can enter in. I will carry thee to that place, where thou shalt see my holiness. The mountains will have to depart, for to you I am the highest. As often as you find a safe gate, I will help you over safely. Your last request or plea I hear. I place on you the crown of life, in airy choruses of angels I will now bring your soul within, here thou shalt be with God forever. I am thy shield and great reward I, Oh Son of God."

So, with God's help through the huge mountains, we arrived in San Marcos on <u>February 14</u> at 12:00 p.m. We left shortly for the huge city named Guadalajara, arriving there at 4:00 p.m. We were now due for a resting period; we were very tired. In this big city, we saw street cars, the same as in the most modern cities in Canada. In this city we were shown a river flowing beneath it, closed in on top and people were walking and driving on the enclosed river. This is supposedly the most beautiful place in Mexico. We were told the temperature doesn't rise higher than twenty-seven degrees Reaumur in summer and not below zero degrees in winter. It was now bedtime, and we thanked and praised our creator for being with us and not leaving us. We had a good night's sleep.

The next morning coming out of my quarters, I met the two old uncles, who were refreshed and happy; they had a good night's sleep. Now all of us were more ambitious and happy. We had no real pain from riding the donkeys. In fellowship, we all ate breakfast, after which we again toured the city, the huge buildings, and the covered river (mentioned earlier). We were not very interested though, because our thoughts were mainly on Mexico City where we were supposed to meet the President. This was very important to us. I also met a German person who wanted to sell me some land, but I was not interested now, because I was not sure we wanted to buy land here. Our privileges of freedom of religion and our faith were more important than land at this time. I asked this person about the weather in Mexico: How much rain did they have, and did it thunder when they had rain? "Yes," he said, "often lightening as if the whole heavens were burning, a great amount of lightning, thunder and very great cloudbursts of rain." I left this friend, for the day had come to an end.

Approximately at 5:00 p.m. we again left on a long train. It was full of many different kinds of people, giving us reason to closely watch our baggage. Upon leaving the city, our thoughts were that we might never see it again. We again travelled through mountains and valleys, past islands and a lot of land that was under cultivation. We travelled all through the night and finally on the 16th of February at 9:30 a.m. we arrived in Mexico City. On our trip, we had seen many grain fields with good irrigation systems, and old areas with very expensive land. We were welcomed in a friendly manner into this huge city that has a population exceeding well over one million. A hotel named Mageskeet was our resting place after the long journey. We were now far south of Canada, where our loved ones were, and how nice it would have been to get a letter. We did a lot of walking around in Mexico City the next day, thinking about the huge undertaking ahead of us. We met Arthur J. Bronof, who was supposed to take us to President Obregon. He had been notified ahead of time by Uncle Johann Wiebe, who had worked with Mr. Bronof and Mr. Lopez earlier. The time passed quickly until we were to meet the President. We were notified by Solis to go see the President on the evening of the 17th but to first go to the man in charge of acreages. We were silent, thinking of what we would say to "Your High Honour," for we didn't want to make any mistakes. We planned who was to present our wishes, choosing Uncle Julius Loewen, with the rest of us helping out where and whenever possible.

The evening soon came, and after preparing, we went to the office of the Minister of Acreages. Together with him, we went with cars to the palace of the President. Arriving at the gate of the yard, we were met by a host of armed soldiers. The Minister drove in first, and we were all granted permission to enter. In the huge courtyard, we were led by armed guards to the palace door where we entered and were seated. We waited awhile, and then the President came. He greeted us warmly and shook our hands, using his left hand because his right arm was missing due to a shooting which occurred years ago. We were asked to be seated and Julius Loewen presented to the President our wishes on paper. We were asked many questions about how we lived, etc. and we answered the best we could. The following is an account or write-up of our interview with the President, which we drew up later in our quarters.

Mexico City, <u>February 17, 1921</u>. The following is an account of our presentation on the above-mentioned date in the palace of President Alvaro Obregon, in the presence of the President, the Minister of Acreages, A.J. Bronof and Daniel Solis Lopez as interpreter.

1. Marriages: The Mexican government had experienced beforehand, that marriages were performed by a minister without both parties being in love. This was disapproved of by the Government, and so a rule was enforced that a judge be present in the house of the couple wishing to wed, with both sets of parents in attendance, who were then asked if their children were going to be wed of their own free will. If this was answered with a yes then notice was given for three weeks, one week at a time, or a notice was posted. If at this time no one had anything against their marriage, the wedding was approved. Their rules were strange to us, so we talked them into not interfering with our customs. However, if our newlyweds were to register through the Government, they had to appear before the judge, before or shortly after the marriage. They both had to say that they married of their own free will, then sign papers which were registered, and it would be ruled a marriage. The reasons for these rules were that if later the marriage became illegal, or they divorced, the woman in the marriage that had been registered could claim possessions and be protected by the law. A marriage that is not registered leaves the woman unprotected.

2. The Waisenamt: The President's answer to this was that in order to make it easier for them, they would follow our testament if troubles should arise. They did not have a rule for orphan inheritance. However, if trouble arose, these would rule as follows. They would give heed first to the son, then the wife, then the daughter, etc. It was agreed upon, that when people joined our church and promised to obey the rules of the church, that the Waisenamt rules were included.

3. Schooling: The President gave us permission to have our own schools, teachers and language. He questioned whether it would be reasonable to later learn the country's language. However, when we told him our reasons and explained our experiences and why we opposed this, he praised our solid foundation of beliefs and promised never to interfere or harm us in any way in our schooling.

4. Exclusion from military service: We were granted freedom from joining the military since they chose only Mexican citizens. Should we, however, on our own free will wish to join, we were granted this privilege.

5. Taxes: No definite answer was given to us about tax omission for the first few years. However, they would do their best to help out the new settlers. A more descriptive answer would be given later.

6. Immigration: The immigration of our old, weak, or crippled families would be no problem. This was because the President was crippled at the time his right arm was shot, yet he later became president.

7. Land: We wondered whether the government-owned land was suitable for farming and or agriculture. They said they had such land and we could look at it.

8. Documents: We asked, since we were strangers in this land if they would help us out by obtaining the right papers for land purchases. This was granted.

9. Settling: This time, we were promised help for all our immigrants to get to their settlements from the border. Furthermore, all belongings, be it horses, cattle, machinery, or household goods were duty-free and the cost of transportation was half price. This help would be supplied from the border to the settlement. These were their rules for all their inhabitants.

10. Government: Our tenth and last question was whether these privileges had to first pass through Congress. The President answered by saying that he did not sign any papers that had not already passed through Congress. In the end, with tears in my eyes, I said, "Thank you for the friendly welcome and for granting us our privileges. We will look up to you as a very gracious government, and you will be rewarded in Heaven." The President and the Minister were emotionally moved, and the President stated that we should come to the Republic of Mexico, to live in a beloved land. After an hour and a half, we departed with warm handshakes. The President reminded us that we had found a better welcome here than in any other land or country that we had already been to.

After our farewell to the President, a servant came out of another room and bid us farewell also. We were astonished at his uniform, with the shiny decorations on his shoulders, etc. In friendship, he offered to show us everything in this huge palace. We went onto the second floor, and he showed us the Mexican coat of arms, an eagle holding a snake with its beak and claws. After showing us around for a while, he informed us that it wasn't very convenient to show us the rest of the palace. However, he informed us that if we came back the next morning, we could have a better look at the palace. We agreed and went back to our quarters. We praised and thanked Him, who can rule and lead the hearts of Your Highness (the President), according to His holy will. This we felt truly of the President and Minister of Acreages (1 Kings 10:6-9).

On the 18th of February, we all woke up healthy and happy. At 11:00 a.m. we again walked to the President's palace. At the gate, we informed the soldiers why we had come. The servant met us at the door and showed us the rest of the palace and all the worldly goods that a President in this world possesses. I thought of the President's riches, but I was more concerned about our privileges. If only we could get them according to our requests, that would be our heartfelt wish. Worldly riches will in time decay, and happiness to the President and other kings will be eternal riches. Revelation 21:24. We walked around a lot in the city, to make time pass. We saw the beautiful flower gardens the Mexicans had made, with many different kinds of plants and some had bouquets for sale. We wandered onto a street called "Lions Street," where a white lion lay on both ends of the street. They must have been monuments of long ago, of which there are many in Mexico. Today we had a good thunder shower. We saw several American planes flying overhead.

February 19, 1921. We awoke healthy, and we are still in Mexico. If all the documents are ready, we will leave tomorrow. We again walked around the city. In a house we saw four meteorites that had fallen from the sky, so they told us. One weighed 28,980 pounds. They looked like stones. The days seemed longer and longer. We decided to send a telegram home to find out if all was well there. They were happy to receive word and all was well at home.

February 20, 1921. The next day was Sunday, and we held a service in our hotel room. Minister Julius Loewen spoke. After dinner, we drove out of the city close to the mountains. At the bottom of the mountains was a beautiful place of small rivers and islands. This place was given to the workers of Mexico City so they could live off it. One island was planted with this and another with that, and all had many flowers. The islands were small, about fifty feet by one hundred feet, although some were a bit bigger. We could see snow in the distance on the mountains. We also saw a distant volcanic mountain. However, to get a closer look at it meant riding a horse or a donkey a whole day just to get there, so we didn't go.

Today is February 23 and we are still in Mexico City. The weather is warm between five to eight degrees. Yesterday, February 22nd, was a holiday so our paperwork rested on the table. We again talked to Mr. Bronof, and were told in twenty-four hours it would all be ready. It seemed like a long time to wait to us.

February 25th, we woke up in good health and praised the Lord for it. The whole day was spent with our papers, which requested freedom in our schools, etc. Our documents were prepared, but as for schooling, we were required to learn and teach Spanish also. This we did not approve of since we thought or understood that the President had given us all rights of schooling, including the language. He had mentioned that it might be helpful for us to learn the language, for it might be useful in the future. Should we ever come before the courts, our language would not be approved of. We told them the Spanish language would hinder our young people, and that up until now, our Mennonites had learned only the German language. He again approved of our solid foundation. We could not believe that after receiving promises of freedom in our schools, it had been changed within the documents.

We asked Mr. Bronof whether we could again speak to the Minister of Acreages, who had been with us when we talked to the President. He, however, wanted to go ahead of us. We followed and were again allowed to present our wishes. Uncle Johann Wiebe sat close to the Minister and explained our situation as best he could. It wasn't long before he consented to our wishes to teach German only in our schools, and we left shortly after in hopes that finally our wish would be granted. We went back to get our tickets for the trip back home, however, we wanted to look at land in Durango.

On February 26th, we again awoke in good health. There wasn't much we could do about our paperwork. Time moved slowly for us, but the people were helpful and always ready to show us around to see something new. Even though we were not interested we went with them. A certain Mr. Wolf showed us points of interest. We again travelled out of town and saw a dairy farm that had twenty-five Jersey cows. These cows were always fed in the barn, and the owners said he usually cleared one thousand pesos a month from these cows. It has become cloudy and we are preparing to leave tomorrow. The President had wanted to see us once again, before we left, but was too busy.

We left Mexico City on February 27, 1921. Mr. Bronof promised to send the documents to Durango, to a hotel where we would be staying, the Hotel Mageskeet. We travelled all day, and Daniel Solis Lopez was with us once again. We went through a tunnel for a long time. The next day we reached Sakatica (Zacatecas). It has lots of flat land, red earth, and hardly any grass or trees. At one time the Mexicans said we were supposed to look out on the other side of the train windows, for we would see fine gardens. We soon saw beautiful gardens with irrigation. Not long after we came to a big city with many people. We travelled on, and nighttime soon arrived. Upon going to bed, Mr. Julius Loewen discovered his suitcase was missing. No use looking for it, for it had been stolen. Finally, we came to the big city of Durango.

March 1, 1921, we went in search of land in three automobiles. By night time, we had gone as far as Conatlan, where we spent the night. The next morning, we travelled north, coming to a big valley with lots of plain level land. We drove alongside a lake, and the further north we travelled, the better the land was. Now and then we saw a river, some with good water. Close to the lake, there was lots of grass and the soil was lighter. Overall, there was good grass, big gardens with fruit trees, and lots of horses, cattle, mules, donkeys, sheep and goats. We were always heartily welcomed while we viewed the land. We thought this was good enough for us, and Mr. Bronof wanted to buy it for us. Actually, Mr. Bronof thought of asking the ranchers, whether they would like to sell. However, we decided not to buy just yet and wanted to look at more land first. We thought of our congregation at home and wondered what they would say about our visit with the President and about the rules regarding freedom in our schools. When we travelled back, we saw more good land, just as suitable as what we had seen yesterday.

March 4, 1921. We awoke in good health, having stayed overnight in Conatlan and saw ranches and good land, mentioned earlier, southeast of town. We saw a big field of winter wheat, just as good as the best wheat back home. We also saw gardens with many kinds of fruit, except bananas. One of the ranches we saw had 75,000 acres, and 73,690 was with good irrigation. From here we travelled to another ranch. They also had good land which lay on the west side of the railroad. We went back again to Durango, arriving at 5:00 p.m. We had left our luggage with the hotel owner and all was in good order.

We had a restful night and once again the next day we all went to see more land. The first land we looked at was at Poonos. From there we walked two miles to a ranch, and from there we rode on a wagon and two horses. Our driver only had small mules, which could only go three-quarters of a mile on a very sandy road. It seemed impossible to continue. We agreed to go back. Back at the ranch, we had dinner and then went back to town. At the ranch, we saw very good soil, trees, grass and a big fruit garden. This ranch has approximately 65,000 acres, and the owner told us the ranch had started in 1731, and had many people living on it. Out on the field, we saw many teams of horses and mules plowing with a share plow. I went over to one team and asked the man whether I could try my hand at plowing. He stepped aside, and I tried my best to hold the plow, but I couldn't plow the way the Mexican could. The wells were ten feet deep and all the land was under irrigation. We arrived back in the city but had to wait for the train. We sat down in the post office, which was only a little mud brick house, with no window. The only light that came in came through the door. It was warm in this house. I told myself if I ever moved to Mexico, I would live in a wooden house because I did not like the smell of the one we were in.

Arriving back in Durango, we went back to where we had stayed earlier. In the evening, we went to the city governor and told him that we had seen good land in the province of Durango. We told him how we had talked to the Mexican President about our freedom of living, schools, Waisanamt, etc., and that these freedoms had been granted to us. He explained that these freedoms would also be upheld here, but the Waisanamt (orphan organization) would leave it up to us, except they requested the names of the leaders, just in case someone else showed up and claimed to be a leader. We thanked them again wholeheartedly for welcoming us, and Mr. Julius Loewen again extended our appreciation.

The governor would have liked to talk to us some more, but he had no more time. He also mentioned that he was sorry that we were seeing the remains of a rebellion in the country. Train cars had been burned, and here and there were huge piles of debris. Before we left Durango, we received our papers of freedom, sent by Mr. Bronof. One set of papers for each: for Manitoba, Swift Current, and our congregation at home.

On <u>March 6th</u> at nine o'clock in the morning, we left the city of Durango in good health. Uncle John Wiebe accompanied us to El Paso. We arrived in Torreon at 7:30 in the evening three and a half hours late due to delays. We had to wait in that city until two o'clock at night before we could board the train that came from Mexico City.

Travelling very slowly, with many delays, we finally arrived at noon in El Paso on <u>March 8</u>, after twenty-four hours. We let someone take us to the border but were unable to cross because our passports had not been stamped by the American Consul in that city. We had to wait quite a while before he came to his office. When he finally arrived it took him quite some time to decide what he wanted to do. But there was another, in a similar position, who seemed to come to our aid. The problem seemed to be the state, or that particular part, did not want to let Mennonites in. But we only wanted to travel through. He asked if we had travel cards. "Yes," we said and showed them to him. Then it was different. He charged $10.00 for each of us, completed our papers and let us go. So we came to the border and could cross shortly. They examined our baggage thoroughly and took some out. I had bought two canes of sugarcane to take home, but they would not let me do so. These were minor hindrances and we could cross the border safely. We left El Paso at ten minutes to nine o'clock in the evening. Some letters from home reached us in El Paso and were eagerly read with longing and yearning. There was one letter, though, we were sorry to receive and gave us no joy. We had to see that once again the enemy in our congregation was not at rest, and sometime later took the opportunity to, unforgettably, make a tear in our members.

Yes, we were now sitting on a different train than in Mexico. Even though they had given us good transportation overall, and we had gotten used to the Mexican ways among the people; it is, nevertheless, completely different from the borders in the States, as if he is in Canada. We travelled even farther north on the Rock Island Railway. At Santeroca there was some snow, but the trees were green. The trees are called evergreen. By noon the snow was gone, and the winter wheat was a nice green. It looked like the land was light soil. By evening, we were in Kansas. All of a sudden, a father with his daughter came into our car; a Mr.

Heinrich Reimer. They were on their way to see a doctor, for the daughter, in another city. They were of the Kleine Gemeinde, as they were called. This meeting was so sudden—a meeting of such old-fashioned Mennonites. Also, their speech was very much like ours. They were very sorry they had not known when we would be returning, or they would have invited us to stop over in Meade. They were very interested to know how we had made out in Mexico and with what results. The loving God knows how to preserve His own; even in the United States.

On the 10th at 7:15, we arrived in the big world city of Kansas City. It rained all the way from Kansas City to St. Paul; much water and green fields. In Des Moines, also a large city, we had to wait several hours. We ate supper. On the 11th we all got up, healthy and arrived at 7:00 in the morning, with an overcast sky. The river was not yet frozen. With the street rail "Street Car", we drove to Minneapolis. It took about 30 minutes. These two great cities are side by side with no space in between. Then we ate our noon meal. In the evening only three of us travelled on; Mr. David Rempel, Benjamin Goertzen, and myself. The others left from St. Paul to Gretna, Manitoba. In Emerson, it was quite cold.

With God's help, we arrived in Winnipeg at 8:30 in the morning. It was quite cold. Mr. David Rempel left at 3:45 in the afternoon for his home, and we had to wait until 10 o'clock in the evening. The next day, the 13th of March, at 2:45 in the afternoon, we arrived in Saskatoon. From there we went, by train, to Warman. It was Sunday and Mr. Isbrandt Friesen met me at the station and took me home. At home, they were all healthy. The Lord be thanked many times. And so, we had made this important and significant journey.

Even though we sometimes had to wait for long periods of time, we really had nothing to complain about; always being in quite good health, "except at the beginning, the likeable director", and good news from home always arrived. Our loving families were in good health and this always gave me new strength and courage so that we were not so unduly weary. Great homesickness we all had to endure, especially in the evening when we were so alone and thought over our day. We were so far from home, surrounded by strange people, who oftentimes watched us in astonishment when we were working together, but they did us no harm. It is something special that we experienced. Therefore, we must thank and praise the Lord forever and ever.

And so I close with this poem when he says (poet unknown):
How good it is to journey with Jesus
Have I not felt in childish time?
He has from one place to another
Brought me safely from here and there.
And so now in this hour
Brought me home in fresh good health.
My Jesus, for this safe journey
Shelter, support, help and good escort...
Give I Thee back praise and thanks
From now and till eternity.
Thine will I, as I am Thine
With body and soul be thine alone.
I am a pilgrim here on earth
Oh when then my pilgrimage
As wished, can end...
Through Your blood, strength and power...
That out of this world's danger
I come to the Lamb's marriage supper with joy.
In that, O Lamb, not from me to take,
I come into Your house.
Shelter, love and grace stand by me.
Lead me surely in and out.
And lead me surely through this world...
To You, my Lord in heaven's vault.
Amen.

This is the end of my grandfather's journal as he travelled to Mexico to scout out the land in preparation for the Old Colony move to Mexico.

Here now are some of the writings of my great half-uncle Isaak M. Dyck who was the bishop of the group that actually moved there.

Thirteen

WRITINGS OF BISHOP ISAAK M. DYCK

Bishop Isaak M. Dyck.

UNREST AND WARTIME

It did not take long before restrictions on our freedoms were introduced. Soon the congregation had to pay large sums of money to the Red Cross. And even if we weren't supposed to regard it as contributing to the military or war effort, it was money that went to strengthen the war effort all the same, a fact that was cause for serious reflection in the hearts of many well-meaning people. Few years had passed since the war had started and already one began to read in the papers that there was to be a general registry throughout all of Canada, from which the Mennonites were not going to be exempted. This war—the great European war—that broke out in August of 1914, was the cause of the registry.

And when in December of 1916 it was announced that these registration cards, which were demanded by the government, had to have all twenty-four questions answered and filled out, the concern grew and became more general and the question of whether this might be the beginning of mandatory military service was seriously considered. It was because of this fear that the decision was reached by the entire congregation not to fill out the cards. Regarding this matter, all of the brothers were called to a meeting in the church at Reinland where it was unanimously decided not to fill out the cards. Some were glad and felt light in their consciences that the congregation was unified and reached a decision collectively. But what happened next? As we were on our way back from the brotherhood and were on our way to Ohm Peter Harms for lunch, the registrar Bennett, as I recall, had already come to inquire about the outcome of our consultation. And as the dear Aeltester Ohm Johann Friesen explained in few words that, on that present day, more than five hundred brothers from all three congregations had gathered and had unanimously determined not to fill out the registration cards, this man's friendly countenance was replaced by a dark expression. He asserted that we would find no reasonable objection not to fill out the cards and that if we would not do it of our own free will, then we would be persuaded by the law to comply. Finally, the man asked the Aeltester and all the other Ohms why we were so afraid to fill out the cards. Aeltester Johann Wall (who was the designated speaker) answered that we were afraid that by filling out the forms we would thereby be pulled into military service. And we were afraid that if we offered our heretofore gracious government but a finger in this matter, they would take the whole hand. To this, the registrar calmly replied that this registration in no way implied such consequences for us, but rather, was only a general census of the people to get an estimate, in order to make a calculation of how many people of each sort were in the country, and he even appealed to the passage in the Gospel of Luke, in the second chapter, where it is written: "In those days Caesar Augustus issued a decree that a census should be taken in the entire Roman world (this was the first census that took place while Quirinius was governor of Syria). And everyone went to his own town to register. So Joseph also went up from the town of Nazareth in Galilee to Judea, to Bethlehem the town of David, because he belonged to the line of David. He went there to register with Mary, who was pledged to be married to him" (Luke 2:1–5). With this, the man said, "If Mary and Joseph would take part in the census, why won't you?" The Aeltester and ministers were silent; they didn't know how to respond, so they asked the man for permission to call another meeting of the brotherhood to discuss the matter again. He readily agreed to this and with a friendly handshake bid them farewell and left hoping to see his wish fulfilled.

On the following Sunday, the brethren were once again summoned to the church in Reinland. Again, a unanimous decision was reached, but this time in favour of filling out the registration cards. It was decided that, as far as our human judgment was concerned, we had no reason not to comply with the wishes of this government representative; rather we desired to do what the government requested of us. However, the Sommerfelder congregation was not at peace with this decision and so decided to send a delegation to Ottawa to inquire about a secure decision. This delegation consisted of the following persons: Aeltester Ohm Abram Doerksen, of Sommerfeld (Manitoba); Aeltester Ohm David Toews, from Rosthern (Saskatchewan); Preacher Ohm Heinrich Doerksen, of Niverville (Manitoba); Benjamin Ewert, of Gretna (Manitoba), and Klaas Peters, from Herbert (Saskatchewan). After a twelve-day absence, these men returned with the happy news that they had been most pleasantly received by the federal government. They also brought back with them a response to these questions the Aeltester answered that the issue was not the language but the fact that it was impossible for us to allow our children to be raised under the flag and under the enthusiastic expression of military zeal. And finally, the Aeltester asked the inspector if he himself didn't believe that the school of today represents the church of tomorrow. Yes, he replied, but he added that it would take about ten or twenty years to come into effect. To another, the Aeltester asked what the true meaning of flying the flag above the schools meant, if not the same thing that it meant when it was raised above the battle-fields, to which the official had to concede a begrudging "yes."

But all of our protest was in vain. How often the Aeltester returned anxious and dejected from Winnipeg where he had gone to seek counsel, and how often in the Thursday assembly of the brotherhood he said to the Ohms that our situation was indeed very sad for all of the lords, regents, and rulers of the land seemed to have turned their looks of friendly approval away from us as if they no longer wished to hear if we complained of our need.

I have already alluded to the extensive monetary offering to the Red Cross that was expected of our congregation during the war, which the government recognized at the time with warm thanks. It was also during the war that the region some seventy-five miles to the west of Morden—the hills of an English settlement called Deloraine—experienced severe crop failure because of a locust invasion. After a plea for assistance was issued to our leaders, we donated about $4,000 and two loads of feed. Our donation was gratefully received and in return, we received many moving letters of thanksgiving. Shortly after this our Aeltester and our Vorsteher, Uncle Johann Rempel, were called to Morden by an official, who may have had a high position in the telegraph service. When he arrived there, this man said he only wanted to thank him for all the help our congregation had given and to say that they wouldn't have made it without us, and if there was ever anything that he could do in return, he would be most happy to do so.

And as things were getting ever worse with the school issue, not only were our brethren being punished with fines and jail time, but the dear minister and servant of the congregation Peter Friesen was sent to Winnipeg as an "evildoer" and was sentenced to two weeks in prison. This awakened a considerable amount of anxiety throughout the congregation, especially because of the time of year—it was springtime, the time when Peter Friesen was supposed to prepare the young people for baptism. I can still remember how many tears were shed and prayers were said on his behalf!

And as the need of the church and the congregation grew ever greater, the thoughts of the Aeltester and Ohms turned once again to this man in Morden who had promised to help us. A delegation drove to Morden to see this man and to present our case to him, and to ask him if he would represent us to the rulers. For as soon as we could find a location, we intended to move away, but in the meantime, we wanted him to ask the government to have patience with us and to give us more time. And he had promised that he would help us if ever he could.

Yes, the man acknowledged, the Mennonites had done much for us, and had donated much money, but this is still not blood. He continued, "I have three sons: one died in the war and is now resting in his grave, the other is somewhere on the ocean on his way there and the third will be sent there shortly so that I will have sacrificed all three of my sons for the war. And the Mennonite sons live no better than ours. Their sons have as much right to be conscripted as our sons do." And this was the sad answer of this man, with which the Aeltester and Vorsteher returned home.

And so the government continued with its school pressure. What made matters worse was that many in our congregation willingly conceded—even desired—to enroll their children in the public schools. They said, "We wish for our children a better education, higher learning than we received." And with this, the foundation for the Tower of Babel was laid. In Genesis 11 it is written, "Now the whole world had one language and a common speech. As men moved eastward, they found a plain in Shinar and settled there. They said to each other, 'Come, let's make bricks and bake them thoroughly.' They used brick instead of stone, and tar for mortar. Then they said, 'Come let us build ourselves a city, with a tower that reaches to the heavens, so that we may make a name for ourselves and not be scattered over the face of the whole earth'" (Genesis 11:1–4).

During this time the people of Canada also began to mock us and yearned to have everything unified under one sceptre, one school, and one language, in order to make for themselves a great name among the nations, and so that in the next war they would be that much stronger. Genesis continues, "Come, let us go down and confuse their language so they will not understand each other" (Genesis 11:7). If we hold up God's Word as a mirror, we will see that we are far from innocent of this

Babylonian idolatry. As Revelation 17:2 states: "With [Babylon, the great prostitute] the kings of the earth committed adultery and the inhabitants of the earth were intoxicated with the wine of her adulteries."

These suspicious tracks could already be seen clearly back then, and this seed secretly grew among us far quicker and stronger than many would believe. For if we still wanted to boast that we were a people set apart, and if we wanted to humbly follow Christ, in spite of the hatred, ridicule, and contempt of the world, there was a lot of pride, exuberance, and arrogance among us, which only made the tower of Babel grow upwards in many of our hearts and homes. It seemed that everyone wanted to be the most honoured, the most educated, and the most respected, and each was trying to outdo the other. And this all came about because some had begun to doubt the command "thou shalt not covet." The great enlightenment with the improved schooling was a net, a dangerous trap, whereby many parents unknowingly allowed their children to be caught. For the enemy, a juggler, a master orator, knew exactly how to convince people that they could comfortably enjoy eating the forbidden fruit. If only he would receive honour, then he didn't mind if the people continued reading God's Word and tried to clothe themselves from head to toe in the dead words. It came to the point where it seemed that everything that was godly had collapsed—people were flying flags not only in the cities, but also in every town, and the powerful zeitgeist threatened to overtake everything. Our situation was just like the one described in 2 Thessalonians, where it says: "He will oppose or exalt himself over everything that is called God or is worshiped, so that he sets himself up in God's temple, proclaiming himself to be God" (2 Thessalonians 2:4).

And with the appearance of holiness, the word of God was partly incorporated as blindness or a larva, behind which the merely natural person would not immediately recognize Satan and be frightened. And it was said: "God's Word is still being taught and the national language will never hurt us." Should God have spoken? (Genesis 3:4). And the decline was already so extensive that many among us could not decide whether to obey the law and send their children to the worldly schools or not. Many said that if only they could send their children to the public schools without the threat of them having to bear arms, then they wouldn't have a problem with it. Because of this sort of thinking, mass confusion erupted, which could only divide us further. It was not only because of this issue that the emigration question arose, but it damaged the congregation in other ways as well. People began to envy their neighbours. There were many who didn't want to hear anything about the worldly schools. Others laughed about it and said: "We can teach the children the Word of God in the churches—we don't need the schools for that. We should feel obligated to obey our rulers." On and on it went like this. All of these dissenting opinions were indicative of a huge rift forming among us. If only we had been of one mind and one heart when we were confronted with the school question, then the government would have been forced to say: "Yes, there is a worthy people." And the dear Lord would have let us enjoy the favour of the citizens of the country, so that we may have been able to stay a while longer in peace and quiet in Canada.

The people of Israel were once in a situation very similar to ours. If they had stood in obedience before God and had followed his ways and his laws, then they would have been privileged among other peoples, as we read in Deuteronomy 4: "See, I have taught you decrees and laws as the Lord my God commanded me. Observe them carefully, for this will show your wisdom and understanding to the nations, who will hear about all these decrees and say, 'Surely this great nation is a wise and understanding people.' What other nation is so great as to have their gods near them the way the Lord our God is near us whenever we pray to him? And what other nation is so great as to have such righteous decrees and laws as this body of laws I am setting before you today? Only be careful, and watch yourselves closely so that you do not forget the things your eyes have seen or let them slip from your heart as long as you live" (Deuteronomy 4:5, 6–9). This was, however, because of our decline, no longer possible. Therefore, the words of our Saviour are that much more relevant: "Every kingdom divided against itself will be ruined" (Matthew 12:25). Thus it would be impossible for our poor congregation to survive the present confusing situation unless it would renew itself, rouse itself, and through righteous atonement and a change of heart seek to live a better life, which would be evident through the fruit borne by the congregation, and through which we would demonstrate that we "hold unswervingly to the hope we profess, for he who promised is faithful" (Hebrews 10:23). And yet the emigration question became ever more serious, so much so that I often heard the dear Aeltester Ohm Johann Friesen saying that it was high time to flee and to "humble [our]selves, therefore, under God's mighty hand" (1 Peter 5:6).

It wasn't only because of the school issue that we began to consider leaving Canada. It was also because we were becoming too much like the world—because of the automobiles and the ostentatious clothing. And the only thing that could preserve our simplicity in Christ would be if we were to again take up the walking stick. But where would we go? Again, the brotherhood met with great anxiety and many tears, and through prayer and supplication sought guidance, and we discussed at length with the brethren how we wanted to do this. In fact, in total, twenty-one meetings of the brotherhood were called to discuss the topic of emigrating. And so you see, my dear children, moving from one land to another is not an insignificant matter.

And it really was high time to move, because many of our brethren were becoming sleepy and indifferent, and began to comfortably eat the forbidden fruit along with our mother Eve. If the Canadian government had not taken such an aggressive step by saying that it wanted to make us all into one hundred percent Canadians, I am convinced that most of our congregation members would have stayed in Canada. This seemed to many to be a risky situation, so when the dear Aeltester Ohm Johann Friesen finally asked at a meeting of the brotherhood how many were in favour of moving, the answer was unanimous—everyone wanted out! Many brothers expressed their desire for us to find another country where we could have total religious and educational freedom and still be able to make a living, even if we couldn't accumulate the same earthly treasures that we were able to in recent years in Canada. Many of those who had come under the most pressure regarding the school question thought only of the words of the apostle Paul when he said: "But if we have food and clothing, we will be content with that. For we brought nothing into the world, and we can take nothing out of it" (1 Timothy 6:8, 6).

But there were many who did not share this sentiment, for many looked with high hopes and great expectations to the future. And so the goal of our wandering—the land far across the Atlantic—Argentina, in South America, a rich and fruitful land, good for growing wheat, shone with the promise of continued economic prosperity. But we were not thinking of the words of the prophet Isaiah, who, speaking for the Lord, says: "'My thoughts are not your thoughts, neither are your ways my ways,' declares the Lord. 'As the heavens are higher than the earth, so are my ways higher than your ways and my thoughts than your thoughts'" (Isaiah 55:8).

"The precious cross alone makes a precious Christian." A very thought-provoking finish to my excerpts from Bishop Isaak M. Dyck's writings.

Quoting also from Delbert Plett's book *OLD COLONY—Mennonites in Canada 1875-2000*, pages 127-128:

"The 1950's.

In his writing, Aeltester Isaak Dyck described these early years in detail.

Because the whole ministerial had emigrated, the official Reinlander Church (another term for Old Colony Church) no longer existed in Manitoba. Isaak's oldest brother, Johann Loeppky, who was the son of Maria and her first husband Johann Loeppky, became a minister [actually ordained as Bishop March 20, 1930, author's note] in the Reinlander church [later known as Old Colony Church] in the Hague-Osler area in Saskatchewan.

In 1948 Johann Loeppky also moved to Mexico with a group of Mennonites who left this Northern Saskatchewan area and settled on the fringes of Manitoba Colony near the border of the Kleine Gemeinde Quellen colony. Numerous families were attracted to Rev. Loeppky's area. But the younger brother and Aeltester Isaak M. Dyck excommunicated those settlers. The area was abandoned and Johann Loeppky ended up back in Canada.

CONCLUSION:

Aeltester Isaak Dyck was a member of a community that emigrated from Canada in 1922. Therefore the perspective of his memoirs is of someone who experienced the exodus firsthand. But he was also one of the leaders. It was his understanding and guidance that structured the community development in Mexico. He had a particular worldview that stemmed from his personal theology. Although the church ministerial acted as a team, it was the leadership of the Aeltester that determined the direction. This form of theocracy was difficult to continue in a democracy such as Canada.

In northern Mexico, the Mennonite leadership exercised more control over its people. Some of these isolationist ideas made life economically challenging for the majority of conscientious villagers. His concern regarding the spiritual vitality of the people was genuine, but his theological perspective determined that more than any other influence.

Isaak M. Dyck was a family man, but most of all, he was dedicated to the Reinlander church. He is remembered as the Aeltester that struggled to make this Mexican landscape a spiritual home for this 'pilgrim people'.

Isaak M. Dyck died on Dec. 2/1969. He was 80 years old, a true pioneer.

Fourteen

QUOTES FROM 'SEEKING PLACES
OF PEACE'...

Royden Loewen from Steinbach was a professor in Mennonite Studies and he has co-authored the book *Seeking Places of Peace.* He wrote about the Old Colonists' move to Mexico and has a good objective view:

Mexico promised the Canadians complete autonomy over all matters of faith, including military exemption, private church-run education, church marriage, gender-equal inheritance, admission of the handicapped and local government. The Mennonites' part of the deal was simply to come to Mexico to transplant their farming skills, abide by the laws of the land and help modernize Mexico's rural economy.

For the Mennonites, the move was ultimately an act of faith. In his memoirs, Isaak Dyck, an Old Colony minister, revealed that the migrants of 1922 were simple "followers of Jesus...born in sorrow, suffering and persecution" consisting of a church now tested "like gold in a fire so that its...steadfastness would be manifested to the whole world." Canadian wealth had seduced the Mennonites with the lure of "brightly painted houses" and "frenzied commerce," necessitating the "learning of a nationalist language" and only a painful physical separation from this lure could halt their assimilation to the world.

Still, the move was controversial. Many of the migrants returned to Canada, especially during the 1930s following a series of thefts, a drought and an epidemic. In the 1930s the state government enforced Mexico's constitution and temporarily closed the doors to the Mennonites' German language schools. Now settlers considered resettlement in other places -- Quebec, South Dakota, South Africa, Paraguay and even islands off the coast of Australia—that might grant complete freedom of education. Many others reasserted their religious commitment, concurring with the Old Colony minister who reasoned that "if it was right that we left Canada then, it cannot be right for us to return now."

An October 1945 letter by a "Frau Guenther" recalled the argument for remaining in Mexico: Guenther reflected on life back in Hague, Saskatchewan when school officials had encouraged her father to send his gifted daughter away for "a town education." She wrote, "I am so thankful to him and to God that he did not do so for what would have happened if I had gone? What kind of children would I have had; boys who joined the army, girls who would have mocked the old ways?" Canada in the eyes of those who had settled in Mexico was a land of plenty, but one that made it difficult for true Anabaptist descendants to live out a life of humility and peace.

I quote Royden's conclusion on this matter:

"Between the 1870s and 1930s Mennonites in North America dispersed throughout the western portion of the continent. The diversity of religious thought was immense, but a common identity as Mennonites held as in each place they grappled with the meaning of being a follower of Christ in a strange new physical environment. Some communities emphasized an individual spiritual quest, striving for personal peace forgiveness and grace, and guidance in life. Other communities strove for a separation from the wider world, a communitarian community purity and non-conformity that directed them to increasingly isolated places of settlement."

He goes on to say, "Some voices in the United States roundly criticized the Canadians in the south. Historian Harold S. Bender, for example, denounced the Old Colonists' intentional poverty and the rejection of rubber tires on tractors, electricity and cars as a form of 'extreme introversion, regression and degeneration.'

On the other hand, one historian marvelled at their success in surviving in Northern Mexico and their resourcefulness in their various endeavours in agriculture and dairy production."

Continuing, he says, "These virtues attracted about 2,500 Manitoba as well as some Saskatchewan Mennonites southward after the Second World War: about 600 Kleine Gemeinde and 250 Old Colony Mennonites settled in Chihuahua state and about 1,500 Chortizer and Bergthaler Mennonites located in the rainforest of East Paraguay. Heading to Mexico offered an implicit rebuke to the technological advances in North America that helped commercial farmers succeed, but impeded the ways of the humble husbandman."

And here he quotes our grandfather. "In his response to a local newspaper's enquiry in November 1948, Old Colony bishop Johann M. Loeppky of Osler, Saskatchewan, leading a small group of 25 families to settle at Los Jagueyes, Chihuahua, noted 'the drought in Saskatchewan,' but more importantly, 'as old-fashioned Mennonites,' he hoped his group could live undisturbed.

"'In their way of life', (one consisting of simplicity), 'In western Chihuahua', he said in the simplest of terms, 'two cows can keep an average family well supplied with the necessities of life.'

The simple rural life was a condition of true faith according to Loeppky."

(End of my quotes/information from Dr. Royden Loewen and Steven M. Nolt's book: *Seeking Places of Peace*, pages 78-79 and page 95)

Fifteen

MY REFLECTIONS

As I review the work of these two great men, both bishops in the Old Colony Mennonite church; one in Canada (my grandfather Bishop Johann M. Loeppky) and one in Mexico (Bishop Isaak M. Dyck, my great half-uncle), one cannot help but notice the great schism between the same church conference in two different countries. Whereas these (half) brothers had experienced a wonderful "Jonathon and David" relationship as our grandfather referred it to, it all fell apart it seemed, when Uncle Isaak and most of the ministerial moved to Mexico. They projected disapproval of the ministerial in Canada, Bishop Loeppky in particular.

It deeply saddened our grandfather and in my empathy, I wanted to understand what exactly happened to create this big rift. I read my great half-uncle's writings; I really wanted to get behind his motives. First of all, I noted he was a brilliant, well-read man of deep commitment to his faith. But what motivated him to be so dedicated to make the Mexico group the "genuine" Old Colony Church that he ended up excommunicating members who moved close to our grandfather's area wanting to be ministered to by him? Why did this not sit well with Uncle Isaak?

As quoted in his writings above, I couldn't help but notice his constant theme of going through hardships/persecution/simple living/staying with our group/church etc. as being the guidelines for righteous living. This would keep them close to God and therefore guarantee good behavior and loyalty to the church. Excommunication and fear seemed to be the "tools" as it were, to put this into place. But what was it doing to people? And why were they not content to stay in their area, moving instead closer to where our grandfather would be? (I'm referring to his move there in 1948). The excommunication factor was the reason for these people abandoning their desire to be near our grandfather when he would come and therefore moving back. Excommunication was the equivalent of having their names stricken off the "Lamb's Book of Life" and being sent to hell, quite bluntly put! This fear motivation brought the forced obedience which our great half-uncle felt was needed to keep them faithful not just in this case but in many other cases.

Also, the leadership in Mexico was sure that the ones who didn't move to Mexico were not in the Gemeinde (Fellowship) and therefore not in right standing with God. Bishop Isaak Dyck referred a lot to the children of Israel and the troubles they had to endure because of their disobedience.

Here's a thought I had: In regards to the children of Israel, were any of them "left behind"? No, God had them all.

In the Exodus of the Mennonites to Mexico, did any of God's children get "left behind"?

They did NOT! God had them all! SOME of them were in Mexico but SOME of them were also in Canada and the rest of the world!

Sixteen

FROM DARKNESS TO LIGHT IN BELIZE; VERNA AND JAKE MARTENS

Verna and Jake Martens were missionaries to Belize in the sixties and seventies. Here's an example of where excommunication went too far as related by Verna in her book *Beyond our Wildest Dreams*:

More and more men were being excommunicated mostly because of the rubber-tire issue. Every man, except one, had been excommunicated in the village of Neustadt. Anger was getting out of control. Most topics of conversation in the colony revolved around the shunning and banning issue. Everybody in Neustadt knew that it was only a matter of time before the last man in their village would receive his document of excommunication. The men in the village agreed to thoroughly whip the official bann carrier, (the bann carrier was a "vorsteher") when he arrived. One day the horse and buggy approached. The carrier was afraid, threw the document in the yard beside the driveway, and took off. Everybody was ready for him and he did not get very far. The men pulled the carrier off his buggy, stretched him over a barrel and with a V-belt gave him a whipping.

The Old Colony church took this to the police and a court case was pending, just as we (Jake and Verna) were starting to apply for permission to move to the colony. The chief immigration officer and the chief of police asked Jake to meet with them before the case went to court. They were at their wits' end. Permission had been granted for the Mennonites to move into Belize thinking that these were the people that would raise a barn in a day if one of them were in need. In their minds, they had granted permission to a peace-loving people. Now, after seven years, things had gotten quite out of control. The Old Colony leadership had made a request to the government that none of the banned men should be allowed to log trees. The officials, getting rather tired of the Old Colony complaints, cut off all logging, which was a huge blow to the entire colony.

It was in this setting that we requested a move to Blue Creek. Not only was permission granted, but a letter was sent to the Old Colony leadership holding them responsible for our safety. Leadership informed the government officials that they had freedom of religion and this was a religious matter. However, the reply came back from the government officials that the freedom also extended to the excommunicated group. They had the right to bring in a religious leader who would provide the services that had been denied them. This was very difficult for the Old Colony leadership to accept. I believe they were beginning to see that their harsh and unreasonable dealings were now going to hurt them. There was no turning back. There were two groups in the colony and soon there would be three. The bann had lost some of its power. They could excommunicate people, but now the people could join up with a group and a church that was sympathetic to their needs." (End of quote in Verna's book, pages 80 and 81).

Another incident is quite humorous in the telling: the Old Colony people became ingenious in skirting the rules, the one about rubber tires in particular. They were not to have rubber tires even on their tractors, etc. So when the leadership asked if they had their tractors "on steel" they would answer yes: They had parked their rubber-tired tractors on sheets of steel!

Later on in the book she reports that the core Old Colony group gave up and moved, en masse to Bolivia. Their work in Belize, under the sponsorship of the Evangelical Mennonite Mission Conference here in Canada, thrived. More of the middle group joined with them; people were being saved and baptized. The whole community thrived to where it was a modern place complete with a large evangelical church, Christian school, a clinic, a Co-op and a Credit Union. Also, roads were improved and modernized, a beautiful community thriving to this day.

Seventeen
FROM DARKNESS TO LIGHT IN BOLIVIA

REFLECTIONS BY JACK HEPPNER

My wife, Ruth, and I recently spent about eight weeks in Bolivia. The main purpose of our trip was to connect with our children, who work with MCC in a support role in Santa Cruz, and of course our grandchildren. We left on December 16, 2009 and returned on February 11, 2010.

Although the purpose of our trip was not to investigate the alleged rape cases in the colonies in Bolivia, I had a sense that in one way or another, I would be propelled into the vortex of this situation.

I visited the six Mennonite men in the Cotoca prison for about an hour and a quarter to get their perspective on why they were in prison and what they were experiencing there.

On February 8, 2010, I, along with two others made a trip to the Manitoba Colony to speak with the Bishop.

Because my dialogue with the Bishop came near the end of my investigation, I will document briefly what we talked about in that context. Many of the perspectives I had gained by speaking to others were touched on in this conversation.

DIALOGUING WITH THE BISHOP.
H.S. and I had a very civil but forthright conversation with the Bishop. I told him that I was a minister in Canada and was interested in getting

solid information to share with people back home. I told him that the news of happenings in his colony had spread around the world and that many in the North were seriously concerned about the situation. He could understand that and told us so.

The story he told differed remarkably from the story I had heard in the Cotoca prison, which I had expected. According to him, the men now in prison had voluntarily admitted their involvement in the sex crimes and colony leaders had kept them in isolation for a number of days before bringing them to Cotoca in order to protect them from enraged colonists. I told him that the Cotoca prisoners had insisted on their innocence and that they had been forced to confess under threat of beatings, burnings and death. This the bishop denied vehemently.

H. and I pressed the Bishop a number of times during our conversation about our perceived need to get some counselling help for the women who had been raped. We suggested to him that if women who are sexually abused do not get help, they frequently experience various forms of dysfunction later in life. His response was to say that if these women had been violated sexually while drugged, they would have no recollection of the experience and therefore would not need any help either.

I have often wondered about the slack attitude toward sexual abuse. It is not as if they consider it OK, it's just they seem to think the way to deal with it is the abused must forgive, the offender must apologize to the church and that's that.

I asked the bishop where such gross sexual misconduct had come from. He implied that this was a special case involving outside influences and an alignment with evil spirits in order to carry out these evil deeds. I posed the question of whether there was any connection between these rapes and the reports I had heard of rampant sexual misconduct among Mennonites. I asked him to tell me if what I had heard was not true. I then told him what one man in prison had related to me. How that the standard practice for colony youth was to begin drinking on Sunday afternoon, then when they were quite drunk by evening they would go to the end of the village to participate in sex with one another. The bishop did not deny any of this but did lament how the drinking of alcohol had brought a lot of trouble into the colony.

I asked him whether it might not be helpful to offer the young people something else to do in their spare time—perhaps some volleyball, Bible lessons, something to eat, etc. to give the youth something else to do that was pleasurable. He responded by saying that, in spite of a wayward life during their younger years, when these young people come to baptism before they get married, they always promise to leave this wayward lifestyle in favor of a straight and narrow walk. I responded that I thought for some this would in fact work, but that it would be very hard for others to simply turn away from a life to which they had become addicted and therefore would continue on into adulthood with these patterns of life. I suggested that it would be better for the whole colony if these youth had not become addicted to alcohol and sex before their baptismal vows. I told him about having lived in Santa Cruz and how I had connected with Spanish-speaking Bolivians who had reported to me how many Mennonite men used city prostitutes on a regular basis. This too, he did not deny. However, in the end, he insisted that since their forefathers had at one time left Canada in order to maintain things the way their elders had had things, there was nothing they were willing to change to address these issues among their people.

I then queried whether widespread sexual deviancy among Old Colony Mennonites, which he did not deny, could possibly be the root problem that had most recently found expression in more overt kinds of sexual misconduct in terms of rapes using chemical sprays. I do not recall that he responded directly to this idea. As I had heard from other reports, the official colony line that this was an isolated experience inspired by outside forces seemed to be what he was most comfortable with.

I asked him how the truth would ever really come out, especially in light of the fact that the judicial system in Bolivia can be manipulated with money. He insisted that the truth would eventually come out. When I asked him how the colony would respond if, in a trial, the accused were given life sentences, he responded that then the colony would be able to breathe more easily and carry on with life as usual. And the abused women would find their way through quite well in that case.

When I posed the possibility that there might not be enough evidence in court to convict these men, he simply stated that that would be an impossible outcome and he would not even speculate what the colony would do in such a case.

In the end, we parted with a firm handshake and I reminded him that many people outside of Bolivia were praying for all those involved in this situation. Much more was said during our visit but this is the gist of our conversation as I recall it."

(Those looking to find the entire article "Reflections on Bolivian Mennonite Realities" can find it at the following link: https://dora-dueck.com/2010/03/27/bolivian-mennonite-rape-victims-update/ or they can contact me directly at: jackandruthheppner@gmail.com).

REFLECTIONS BY CAMERON DUECK

Cameron has written his travel memories in his book *MENNO MOTO*. His subtitle *A Journey Across the Americas in Search of My Mennonite Identity* says why he wrote it. His determination and adventurous spirit helped him find his roots and all that came with it: the good, the bad and the ugly, as they say. I highly recommend this book. He has somewhat of a summary on page 251: "The farther away from Canada, the more conservative and reclusive it seemed the Mennonites became. I thought of the people I'd met in Mexico. Despite the radical motives for their move there, they were so close to Canada, so connected by family and business to their northern cousins that a strong sense of family remained. In Belize, the Mennonites were a bit farther away, their lives more adjusted to the tropical, Caribbean lifestyle, but there was still a sense of connection. In Bolivia, I'd felt like I was far away from home, and the Mennonites there, while maintaining their Canadian roots, were mostly of a radical, ultra-conservative variety that I had trouble associating myself with. But those in the Paraguayan Chaco went beyond that. From what we'd heard in Canada, it sounded like they'd moved to another planet entirely."

Eighteen
CAUSES OF DARKNESS:
GUILT, FEAR AND MANIPULATION

A deeper study into what guilt, fear and manipulation really are would give us more understanding as to why it should not be used like this. One of our pastors here in Steinbach did a very helpful sermon that he gave me permission to quote. His series was entitled The Intentional Life, and pt 5 "Why You Can't Rest: Guilt & Fear" was the section that we will quote and use here.

God intentionally made us to need rest. "Resting is an important part of being human and pleasing God in its own right. Resting well is part of how we please God because He made us to rest." He's not just referring to the rest we need each night but recreational rest as well. He uses the example of Jesus' baptism. Jesus, already thirty years old at the time has yet to begin His ministry. This is very important because when He comes up out of the water, God pronounces: "This is my Beloved Son, in whom I am well pleased" (Matthew 3:17). He hasn't done anything yet...no disciples chosen, no miracles, no crowds following him and yet God is pleased with Him just because He is His son. What does this mean for us as God's children? Do we feel we have to *do* things for God before He can be pleased with us? And when is it enough?

In the Old Colony world, it was so important to follow the directive of the church leaders; they would set the guidelines for the people to follow. And even though some of these guidelines didn't make sense and were very inconvenient, they tried hard to obey them. According to Bishop Dyck's sermons, hardship and suffering were necessary to bring one closer to God. So they obeyed. But it did not bring peace to the troubled soul. When was it enough to guarantee a place in Heaven? One could never know; it was always only a *hope.*

According to this Steinbach pastor: "It's been so deeply imprinted into our psyches that God could only ever be happy with us when we do stuff for Him. But God's love for us isn't transactional." He goes on to cite the example of a parent (a good parent, that is) completely loving and accepting his newborn baby even though the baby gives nothing in return.

He refers back to his topic of true rest and says, "True rest cannot happen in a life that is constantly cluttered with guilt and fear. True rest cannot happen in the life of a person who thinks they have to earn God's love. Such people can never truly let go and just be, which is what true rest comes out of." He then goes on to talk about guilt and fear and why they are unhealthy motivators in the Christian life.

"Because guilt and fear are real emotions that God has created; they're hard-wired into our brains for a reason. The problem is that many of us have no idea what they're actually created for, and as a result, we try to use them for the wrong things.

"Healthy guilt: a negative emotion you feel after doing something wrong, which motivates you to make things right (then goes away)...It is not a positive emotion that you carry around with you to motivate you to do good things. That is unhealthy guilt. It shows that something is wrong."

If you do good things for "guilt" reasons, then you will eventually end up feeling resentful either to God or the church, church leadership or whoever put this on you. You will also feel worthless and useless and perhaps even "quit" in more ways than one. This pastor says, "Your body and brain were not made to run on guilt...Guilt is a short-term emotion after you do bad things; guilt is not a long-term emotion for motivating you to do good things."

He goes on to talk about FEAR, "Healthy fear: a short-term negative emotion that motivates us to stay away from danger, or mobilizes us to find safety when we get into danger. Fear is a negative emotion created by God to keep us physically safe, and to respond quickly and powerfully when we're in danger.

"Fear is a terrible long-term motivator for doing good things. If it is something you are regularly feeling -- something is wrong. When fear is a regular part of your life, it will damage you mentally, emotionally and physically because our bodies were not built to cope with the long-term stress of constant fear. Fear is something we're meant to feel only in short bursts, and then we get to safety." He goes on to give an example of fear-based parenting, setting overly strict guidelines, etc. This smacks of overprotectiveness, interference, and manipulation.

Much like rules given by a church such as the Old Colony beginnings in Mexico.

He cites the scriptures in 1 John 4:18 but I will start the quote from verses 15-18: "All who confess that Jesus is the Son of God have God living in them, and they live in God. We know how much God loves us, and we have put our trust in His love.

God is love and all who live in love live in God, and God lives in them. And as we live in God, our love grows more perfect. So we will not be afraid on the day of judgement, but we can face Him with confidence because we live like Jesus here in this world. Such love has no fear because perfect love expels all fear. If we are afraid, it is for fear of punishment, and **this shows that we have not experienced His perfect love."**

PERFECT LOVE

Here's an example of how living in this "perfect love" works:

This story (of which there is more than one version) about Bishop Johann Loeppky was told by our cousin Schpitz, a nickname for John K. Loeppky, the son of the bishop's son John. (In other words, the Bishop was Schpitz's grandfather).

One Sunday, Schpitz and some of his friends, all in their teens, were playing catch on a vacant village lot near the home of Bishop Loeppky. Since sports on a Sunday was well known to be wrong, they kept a close watch on the bishop's property. It was understood that if he came out of his house, the game would immediately be over!

Well, he did come out, *and* he headed directly towards them.

"I saw you playing ball. So who's got the ball?"

Obviously, they had been caught, so the person, who had been hiding the ball, produced it. "Throw it to me." So the "culprit" threw the ball to the bishop. He, in turn, pointed to another guy and said, "Here, catch! Let's play some ball!"

That's "walking in His perfect love"!

FEAR OF THE LORD

Another point this pastor made was that "the fear of the Lord has to do with wisdom and knowledge and respect for the damage sin can cause, not fear of being punished." He quotes the scriptures in Proverbs 1:7, "The fear of the Lord is the beginning of Knowledge, but fools despise wisdom and instruction." It's about having the wisdom and knowledge to make good choices. It's about being a wise person who doesn't make stupid decisions that harm himself and other people."

He also talks about people who've been set free of this fear and guilt: "Sometimes it's not a fun thing or a happy thing for them to be free at first...they don't know how to live with their freedom. They have to discover who they are; they have to find their voice. They have to re-learn how to live apart from someone else controlling and manipulating them."

[End of quotes from this Steinbach pastor.]

This has happened to some Old Colonists who found Jesus but without direction and careful nurturing, they were prey to controlling cults.

Without the Holy Spirit to guide us, we can easily sink back into fear-motivated living. The scripture promises that "So if the Son sets you free, you are truly free" (John 8:36, NLT). Another scripture gives us this promise: "For God has not given us a spirit of fear and timidity, but of power, love and self-discipline...[another translation uses the words sound mind]" (2 Timothy 1:7, NLT).

Going back to Bishop Dyck and the ministerial in Mexico: In his great dedication to this goal, no sacrifice was too much. Hardships were to be expected even that of broken relationships which included that of himself and his half-brother. (Brother Isaak was not available when our grandfather came to visit him that last time). It might have caused him deep grief when our grandfather died soon after he came back to Canada, but one can only speculate.

The Bible discourages us from "judging one another" so I want to stay away from that. I myself have experienced much grace in my own life of imperfections. We all do the best we can with what we've been given, as they say. If we have invited Jesus into our lives and given ourselves to Him, His Spirit within gives us the power to produce good fruit. Galatians 5:22-23 (NLT) says, "But the Holy Spirit produces this kind of fruit in our lives: love, joy, peace, patience, kindness, goodness, faithfulness, gentleness, and self-control. There is no law against these things!" The Bible also says, "By their fruits you shall know them." So we must examine "the fruits". I've already shared my grandfather's life and works as he helped the ones left behind in the great move to Mexico. He didn't see them as unwilling to be "genuine" Old Colony by not moving; rather he empathized with their plight: they couldn't because of finances and other reasons. They were not "excommunicated" for this; rather they were ministered to as genuine believers who wanted to follow Christ. Grandfather saw this potential in all he ministered to and extended grace as God had extended it to him.

The Old Colony people in Canada were not excommunicated for having cars (rubber tires) or sending their children to the English schools. (For this grandfather was greatly criticized, especially by the leadership in Mexico). He knew that outward rules would not ensure a godly outcome; only what's in the heart can change our behaviour. And what behaviour was he expecting? He wisely realized that the expectations in Canada would have to be modified from those in Mexico. He was expecting faithfulness to the church but out of a heart towards God and God alone. His messages were very close to evangelical, preaching the goodness of God (it is the goodness of God that leads us to repentance). At the same time, he exemplified this at every turn, with great humility, never using his position or the fear factor to motivate the people.

When we look at the result of fear and excommunication used by the leadership in Mexico, we see much that brings sadness, not to mention shame to be identified with the name Mennonite at times. Rules just didn't bring the righteousness these early leaders were expecting. Rebellion brought bad behaviour: sneaking off to drink, in spite of "the soul-saving steel wheels" (quoting Cameron Dueck from his book, *Menno Moto,* p. 189), incest was rampant (leaders expected repentance but gave no real behaviour-changing guide lines) and thus it continued and was almost expected. Was there excommunication for this? According to Jack Heppner's report, if there was, it was only temporary.

Nineteen

REFLECTIONS ON WORK IN MEXICO/BELIZE VERSUS WORK IN CANADA

I do know that in 2017 when I went to Belize, they were being excommunicated for reading the Bible on their own. People were hungry for assurance of salvation. There are many scriptures emphasizing our surety of salvation but these kind of scriptures were not preached or emphasized. Your salvation was based on your obedience to the church but even then heaven never was a guarantee of it. To say you were saved or born again was prideful. One could only humbly hope. People were studying scriptures such as John 3:16 which reads: "For God loved the world so much that He gave His one and only Son, so that everyone who believes in Him will not perish but have everlasting life." Often they found salvation and were encouraged by these scriptures to rejoice in knowing they would be with Jesus someday based on what He had done for them on the cross rather than their careful obedience to the church rules.

There are many stories of the horrific things that have happened in the many different colonies in Mexico, Belize, Bolivia, Paraguay as well as other countries nearby. I'm thinking in particular of Esther as well as her sister Lisa who have both written books on their experiences in Bolivia. Both of their parents died in separate accidents and left them orphaned as still young children, Lisa being only 16 when they finally, miraculously escaped to Canada. Read Elizabeth Anne (Lisa) Janzen's book entitled *An Opened Gate* to get her full story. She and her husband later became missionaries there under the EMMC conference. Many hungry people came to know Jesus through their ministry there.

People were so hungry for the truth. My own cousin Susanna and her husband were constantly seeking more, travelling to Gemeinde (fellowships) in different countries trying to satisfy their hungry hearts. They finally found Jesus back in Belize and drank in His precious word (all of it, not just what the preachers gave them on Sunday!) Tragically she and her husband were shot at by some local riffraff, from which she did not survive. I met her sons several years later; all of them also had found Jesus.

From an objective standpoint we can see the results of rules that are enforced by using fear, manipulation and drastic consequences such as excommunication. The Old Colony people had a deep respect for their leaders and did everything they could to avoid these consequences. It made sense to Bishop Isaak Dyck to enforce the rules and thereby make these new beginnings in Mexico as godly as he knew how. However, the people experienced FEAR and this fear was used to get obedience and the "genuine Old Colony church" they envisioned.

Is this the way Jesus wanted it? Emphatically no! According to Jesus, fear is the Devil's tool. Jesus always advocated love. Why did some of the Old Colony people move to Bishop Loeppky's area? They knew he operated in love. From him, they would experience empathy and loving guidance. Our grandfather genuinely believed that that's what the leadership in Mexico wanted too. He had been judged by them but he in return held them in high esteem, expecting of them what he expected of himself, the highest value of our faith, that of love.

HUMILITY
Humility was greatly touted in the Old Colony faith; so much so that:

1. You didn't call yourself "born again" or a Christian because you were assuming too much; one could only humbly hope.

2. Do not hold yourself in high esteem. This was carried to extreme in some cases. We as a family wanted to visit our grandfather's

grave and assumed it would have a noticeable marker. However, it did not. We had to go to the local caretaker of the cemetery to look at a map and then finally be able to locate it. The higher your position, the greater should be your humility. We had a deep respect for this.

However, if "humility" takes precedence over truth and love, then it borders on false humility. I'm thinking now of the attitude of the leadership in Mexico. To consider and judge those who did not move as if they weren't actually even Old Colony or part of the fellowship simply because they drove cars and sent their children to the English schools raises some questions:

The very act of judging and condemning seems to me the opposite of humility, is it not? While Bishop Dyck sounds very humble and serious in his walk of faith, there is very little mention of the love of Jesus and less of the Holy Spirit. Unless we have invited Him into our lives to receive salvation and the Holy Spirit's guidance in our lives, we will, sadly, be doing it in our own strength. And then humility becomes pride: pride in our "humility" as it were. This will definitely result in judgement of others who are not walking the "humble path of faith" like we are: A clear indication of false humility or at least humility based on our own human efforts.

Another question: How can man (the leadership in Mexico) decide what actions deserve excommunication (having your name stricken off the Lamb's Book of Life)?

Our grandfather experienced this; it must have been a real shock. He had put his faith in the Mexican leadership, at times asking their advice in matters of choosing other leadership in Canada to help him lead the flock there. No love of Jesus or respect for his position was extended when he came to Mexico. It almost seemed that, if possible, they would have excommunicated him as well!

One can only wonder at this extreme loyalty: was it man-based and therefore more a loyalty to the church than to God Himself? The word of God was used but without love. I can't help but wonder how this saddened not only our grandfather (it was noted that he returned to Canada a very saddened man), but our God Himself.

Having said all this, I want to extend what God wants me to extend: His love and forgiveness. Many throughout history have done what they sincerely felt was right and created devastating results. As a great half-niece of Bishop Isaak M. Dyck, I have been greatly troubled by the results of the strict guidelines he and the early leadership set forth and enforced. It is still being enforced to this day. As much as I regret what the results have been, I know there was much good that happened as well. I respect and admire the dedication Bishop Dyck had to the mission before him. With all humility and on behalf of all those who were spiritually hurt and disappointed, I offer forgiveness. Where the guidance of the Holy Spirit was not sought, I can only challenge **myself** to do so.

As Jesus said: To whom much has been given, much will be expected. I feel I have been given much.

Twenty

MARIA: MOTHER OF TWO BISHOPS

BISHOP ISAAK DYCK'S MEMORY OF HIS MOTHER'S EXPERIENCE:

"So I, too, can only proclaim or share in one part of the old stories of God's glory, and his omnipotence and wonders, for I was born over there in Canada (July 15, 1889: "Alas, my mother, that you gave me birth" [Jeremiah 15:10]). But as soon as I matured and gained understanding, I eagerly loved to hear the dear elders tell old stories. My curiosity was especially awakened by the stories my dear mother would tell me in my younger years, about how she along with her dear parents came across from Russia to Canada how they travelled across the big ocean, and about how they were on the water for twelve whole days. It is no wonder that I listened to such stories with wonder, because in my entire life I had never even seen a ship, never mind an ocean. She told us often about how they travelled on a ship together with the dear Aeltester Ohm Johann Wiebe, and that she had so much faith in her leader in her younger years that she had been totally without worry or care, and was of the opinion that if Ohm Johann Wiebe was on her ship, then it would be impossible for it to sink. But one evening, as a big storm rose on the sea, and the ship—especially in the bow—began to shake, everyone became very afraid. But before she went to bed for the night, she noticed that the loving Aeltester went to every room on the ship where our people were, and encouraged them all to pray that the ship would not sink on the raging waves, and reminded them all of how the disciples were with the Saviour on a boat that was covered with waves, and Jesus was sleeping: "And the disciples went and woke him, saying, 'Lord, save us! We're going to drown!' He replied, 'You of little faith, why are you so afraid?' Then he got up and rebuked the winds and the waves, and it was completely calm. The men were amazed and asked, 'What kind of man is this? Even the winds and the waves obey him!'" (Matthew 8:23–27).

"And this is what my mother said! She said that they all prayed earnestly that the dear Lord would protect and keep them and that the ship wouldn't go down. And the next morning as they awoke, the storm had subsided and the ship sailed on the smooth sea so that it was impossible to imagine that such a storm had taken place the previous night. And they sang a song of praise to the dear God and thanked him with a happy disposition for his goodness and for the miracles that he performs for his earthly children.

"Others went out on the sea in ships. They saw the works of the Lord, his wonderful deeds in the deep. For he spoke and stirred up a tempest that lifted high the waves. They mounted up to the heavens and went down to the depths; in their peril, their courage melted away. They reeled and staggered like drunken men; they were at their wits' end. Then they cried out to the Lord in the trouble, and he brought them out of their distress. He stilled the storm to a whisper; the waves of the sea were hushed. They were glad when it grew calm, and he guided them to their desired haven. Let them give thanks to the Lord for his unfailing love and his wonderful deeds for men. Let them exalt him in the assembly of the people and praise him in the council of the elders (Psalm 107:23–32)."

The *SS Sarmatian* brought Mennonites from England to Canada during their journey from tsarist Russia in the 1870s.

Maria Martens was the daughter of Abraham Martens (1836-1909) and Susanna Neudorf (1836-1917). Maria and her sister Susanna, together with their young husbands joined their parents in pioneering the village of Blumenfeld, (Manitoba) Susanna (1859-1897) was married to Peter Janzen (1854-1920) whose mother was a Driedger.

Another sister, Katherina, married Johann Driedger, Blumenfeld's first businessman.

Maria (1858-1934) was married to Johann Leopki (1850-1882). Maria and Johann Loepki grieved over several children who died in infancy. In 1882, when Maria was again waiting for the birth of a child, her husband Johann was tragically killed in an accident. Her son Johann Leopki, was born later that same year.

In 1883, Maria (Martens) Loepki entered a second marriage with Isaak Dyck, who was the son of Isaak Dyck and Susanna Fehr. Their marriage was blessed with seven children.

Her youngest son, Isaak M. Dyck (1889-1969), was a respected teacher in the village of Blumenfeld. In 1912, Isaak was elected as a minister of the Reinlaender Church. Isaak M. Dyck moved to Mexico in the early 1920's. He and his parents established new homes in the Manitoba Colony where in 1935, he succeeded Johann Friesen as Bishop.

Maria's older son, Abraham (born 1885) was elected as minister in Mexico.

In the meantime, Maria's oldest son, Johann Loepki, had moved with his grandparents, the Martens, to Saskatchewan around 1900. The Driedger family of Blumenfeld, followed around 1904. Johann Loeppky (change in spelling) was elected a minister in the Reinlander Church (later known as Old Colony). In 1921, he was a member of the delegation which, on behalf of three Reinlander groups in Canada, negotiated a Privilegium (list of agreements) with the Mexican government."

Twenty-One

MARIA: MOTHER OF TWO BISHOP
—MUSINGS

As written by her great-granddaughter Maria, (the author, Mari Klassen). As a mother also, I took the liberty to imagine how it was for her to be the mother of these two Bishops. Although she didn't live through all of the following events (she died in 1934), let's imagine what it might have been like for her if she had. Here then, in the <u>possible words</u> of Maria, the Mother of Two Bishops):

"How thankful I was to God for a sweet healthy baby boy who I named Johann after your father Johann Loeppky. He would never know you as he died in a terrible accident with his horses just a few months before your birth. What a sad time that was for me but how blessed I was that I had you, my little Johann to remind me of him. It was only a year or so later that I met your stepfather, Isaak Dyck who wanted to marry me but was hesitant about accepting you. I felt sorry for my little Johann; first not having a father to welcome him when he was born and now? No welcome from his stepfather. I hoped things would change but alas, they did not.

"One day I found you being taken to the barn where you were given the thrashing of your life for no reason and I knew things would never change. I promptly took you by the hand and brought you to my parents and they were more than happy to have you there. I missed my little Johann; you were only six years old. I visited you often...there was no resentment in your heart; you were such a sweet boy, just like your father, my dear Johann, whom I still missed so much. We'd had several babies together but they did not live. God in his mercy saw fit that you did and I wasn't going to allow any harm to come to you, my precious son.

"And then I was blessed with more babies, more sons...the youngest being Isaak, named after his father. I was proud of my children and so blessed that you Isaak had such a godly concern for the young people as you were teaching them. Your heart broke with the rebellion you saw every day...young people not concerned with the church or the holy things of God. You made a strong commitment to be better, to set a godly example at any cost it seems. You were rejected by your peers but were undeterred. I was so proud of you, my Isaak.

"Later when my oldest son was chosen to be one of the delegates going to Mexico to see about land for our Old Colony Mennonites, he came first to Manitoba to say goodbye to us, his family and to gather together with the other delegates before they left from Winnipeg.

"You were with him Isaak, and you spent precious time together bonding in a 'Jonathon and David' relationship, as Johann later stated in his Mexican travel journal. This blessed my mother heart as nothing else could: "How beautiful it is when brethren dwell together in unity..." (Psalm 33:1b), especially my son and his half-brother.

"But then things began to change and I was apprehensive about our move to Mexico; our Dyck family all went but my beloved Johann stayed in Canada. Most of the ministerial moved to Mexico. There were many Old Colony Mennonites who couldn't move: they had no resources left after the fines paid to the government when they refused to send their children to the English schools. This was the very reason we felt we had to move...they insisted on us giving up our German schools... the very essence of our faith...a promise made to us as Mennonites; now broken!

"A time of turmoil it was in so many ways: families separating, successful farms given up after years of building them up...receiving next to nothing in some cases, strife among the leadership not to mention the extreme conditions of this new country. Many wanted to give up and go back to Canada. Some did. My heart was torn. I had to say goodbye to my son and his family not knowing if I'd ever see them again. But I had to be brave for my other family...I did a lot of praying in those first few years. Isaak's family went through hard times too. One of his children (my precious grandson) died soon after we got there. We were not exempt from the sickness and death that all the others were experiencing. But God was with us, wasn't He? My son Isaak, the new Bishop, surely thought so. He preached so much about the Old Testament: trials the children of Israel went through and the punishments they had to experience because they were disobedient.

"I knew about the judgements and criticism projected by the Mexican ministerial towards those who didn't (couldn't) move from Canada, the greatest of these targeting my older son, now a bishop in Canada. He was and always had been a man of empathy and love towards his flock, which he now saw as "sheep without a shepherd". He had such a big heart and couldn't see himself leaving them. There were very few of the ministerial left to help him, but they managed to bring the love of Jesus to the ones left behind. And then in 1948, we heard that Johann was moving to Mexico as well. My mother heart was thrilled to hear it; finally, my sons would be together again! I had heard the desires of many here in Mexico; how they longed for him to come too. Maybe he would have influence over his younger brother and the rules would be softened to be more bearable.

"But it was not to be so. My Isaak heard these rumblings too and was more determined than ever to stay the course. This was going to be genuine Old Colony and no compromising of rules would happen on his watch. In fact, when he found out some were moving into the area where his half-brother was going to be, he promptly excommunicated them! Furthermore, he warned all those who wanted to be in Loeppky's church, that they would be excommunicated as well.

"I welcomed my oldest son with a sad heart, wanting to warn him of what was to come. But I didn't; I could only pray. Pray that the 'Jonathan and David' relationship would be restored, that there would be that sweet harmony once again. But alas, as time went on, I saw that this was not going to happen.

"My carefree, happy son Johann was met with rejection once again: people had been threatened to stay away from his preaching...clearly, he was not wanted! He left after only a year or so, trying one last time to meet with his brother to set things right. That was always his heart; he wanted no animosity, no misunderstanding between them. Sadly, his brother was unavailable. He tied up all other loose ends and left for Canada, a saddened man. I was sad too; maybe I would never see my precious Johann again!

"As it was, he died in August of 1950. His newest granddaughter Anna was only 6 months old. I never did see him again or any of his family in Canada.

"Why could things not have been different? Why must you be so harsh to your brother, Isaak? Your older brother, no less. How nice it would have been to be in harmony together, to be modified in your stance. You see how the people felt towards Bishop Loeppky; they were craving his kind heart and gentle dealings. Why don't we seek the Lord together and ask how He wants to lead His people? Isn't there a better way to bring obedience to their hearts? Rules don't change a person's heart and forcing them to obey by threats of excommunication won't make a genuine change either. The Bible talks about the grace of God and how Jesus died so that we could live for Him. He sent the Holy Spirit to live within us so we would have the power to obey Him. Why don't we have more preaching about that? My heart longs to hear more about His saving grace and I believe many of the others do too. But, I can only pray.

"Perhaps my prayer will be answered when we get to heaven: there I see Jesus greeting both my sons with, 'Well done, good and faithful servant.' I see Him placing your hands together and blessing again your 'Jonathon and David' relationship.

"There finally, we will live in harmony and peace forever."
Amen!

CONCLUSION

In these writings, I've tried to show that *A Dim Light* is still a light. Our life in the Old Colony setting merely pointed us to the Light. However, it was "dimmed" almost into obscurity by the ever-present rules and expectations of what spiralled into a man-orchestrated religion. For some, it was enough. But for others it was more the arrow to follow in finding the brightness of this Light—Jesus and the freedom only He could bring.

Where the focus was more on Jesus as the Light, the people's lifestyle reflected this; for example the acceptance extended to us and other denominations as shown by my Driedger cousins in La Crete. Where the focus became more the enforcement of rules (the "Ordnung" which in some cases trumped the Scriptures), the Light became dimmer.

The contrast is too great and our hearts should be moved into action. I could not just enjoy the Light and Freedom I have found and ignore what "my People" in darkness have and are still experiencing. If these writings can help even one person find Jesus and all the forgiveness, freedom, and joy He offers; then praise God, I have done as He asked of me.

I close with these verses from 1 John 1:5-7 (NLT):

> "This is the message we heard from Jesus and now declare to you: God is Light, and there is no darkness in Him. So we are lying if we say we have fellowship

with God but go on living in spiritual darkness; we
are not practising the Truth. But if we are living in
the Light, as God is in the Light, then we have fellowship with each other, and the blood of Jesus, His Son,
cleanses us from all sin."

And like my Great-Grandmother might have said, there in Heaven
with Jesus, we will finally live in peace and harmony with each other.
Amen!

EPILOGUE

To be excommunicated because of reading/studying the Bible, how far from the truth is this? It must sadden our Heavenly Father. Bishop Loeppky would have been horrified and even Bishop Dyck, I believe.

But the Friesen family in Shipyard, Belize continued faithful in their new found assurance of salvation and God is always faithful when His word is believed. Henry and Tina Redekopp were in Shipyard as pastors and radio pastors from 2009-2018 and they have this to say about this family: "Dr. David and Aganetha (Nettie for short) Friesen exemplified forgiveness towards the colony leadership. Although their excommunication set back their practice by 80% and cut off the majority of their relationships, they extended grace to those who rejected them. Their influence in the colony continued, although much of their outreach was done by dark and in secret."

When we were there in 2017, the EMMC church was barely half full and only a handful or so of students in their Christian school. But several Old Colony men went to a men's retreat in the area and came back gloriously saved. Shipyard has undergone a radical change since then and I will quote Lyn Dyck Executive Director of EMMC missions in his report:

"Lately the Shipyard church has been having about 250-300 in attendance. Sometimes more for special events...

"Its ministry is primarily to Old Colony Mennonites and in the past couple of years has quadrupled in size. Incredible how God is at work. My colleague just returned this week from providing another leadership workshop to 42 people from this church. Plans are to build a new church and School to keep up with the growth. Our Belize region of churches is also hiring a Regional Pastor Coach to help mentor and disciple pastors and assist in their Ministries. Over the years, Belize churches have been able to hire mostly local homegrown pastors for their leaders..."

WHAT CAN WE DO?
When we came to Belize the first time, I was outside the EMMC church in Spanish Lookout and sensed strongly that this is what my grandfather would have liked to see happen...the gospel freely preached. I knew we were going to Shipyard the next day and it was still very Old Colony. So I asked God, "What can I do? I can't preach there but I know I can pray." When we got there, Henry Redekopp, the radio pastor, asked me to give my testimony on the radio, in Low German! At the end of those two weeks, I gained some confidence in my Low German and so I did it. He said the Old Colonists weren't allowed radios but many of them had them and would be moved by this testimony. Here was the answer to, "What can I do?"

Lyn Dyck also cites ways we can help: "If people would be interested in providing pastoral support funds, or Cornerstone Christian School Tuition support, they can connect directly with www.emmc.ca/donate."

Johann Loeppky and his first wife Anna Neudorf

This picture was taken just before our grandparents moved to Mexico in 1948. The house in the background was built by him, which our mother (and we as well) grew up in; now given to her as an inheritance when he sold everything to make this move. My aunts and uncles from left to right: Gerhard and Sarah (Martens) Loeppky, Peter and Helena (Wiebe) Loeppky, Abram and Agatha (Miller) Loeppky, Jacob and Sarah (Unrau) Loeppky,

Jacob and Helena (Loeppky) Driedger, Johann and Anna (Klassen) Loeppky, Heindrich and Margaretha (Friesen) Loeppky, Abram and Maria (Loeppky) Derksen…our parents. Missing: Johan and Anna (Loeppky) Rempel, already moved to Mexico. Also missing: Isaac Loeppky who took the picture. In front and sitting: Helena and Bishop Johann Loeppky (our grandma and grandpa).

Also taken at the time of Bishop Loeppky's departure to Mexico. The grand-children (my cousins): The tall boy in the back is our brother John Derksen. The three taller girls are two of Johann Loeppky's and one is our sister Helena (bending over me in the white dress with little brother Isaac beside me. Back to the left is Johann Leoppky's Jake. The two girls in front of our brother John are Nettie and Helen Driedger. The little boy looking to the side is Will, son of Peter Loeppky and his sister Katharina is right behind him. The lady bending over is our aunt Anna Loeppky. The rest are Abram Leoppky's, Heinrich Leoppky's and Jacob Driedger's boys. As well there are more of Abram Derksen's boys and one girl (me).

Village of Reinland drawn by our mother during her growing up years.

Village of Reinland drawn by our brother John during his growing up years.

February 2014. My siblings from left to right: Abe, John, Helen, Anne, Mari (in back), Bill and Ike (on far right). - Photo taken by Kevin Olfert

Picture of Ruben and Mari Klassen's family, taken July 10, 2022 at our daughter Maria's wedding. From left to right: (back row) Menno Unger (Melissa's husband), Ruben Klassen (my husband), daughter Maria and Murray Haggerty (bride and groom), Mari Klassen (me, in hat), sons David and Nathan Klassen, (front row) Melissa (now Unger), her daughters Gabbey and Whitney (missing is her eldest daughter Taylor), Jonas (Nathan's son), Nolan (David's son), Gemma (David's daughter), lady beside her is Stephanie (Nathan's wife) and Jodi (David's wife). In front sitting down is Tobin (Nathan's son) and Joelle (David's daughter) and Meg (Nathan's daughter). – Photo taken by Jodi Klassen

Mari and Ruben Klassen. Photo taken by Jodi Klassen.

LIST OF RESOURCES

1. Permission from Lyn Dyck to quote from his report on the work of the EMMC in Belize. (See Epilogue)
2. Permission from Aganetha Friesen, her testimony
3. Permission from Jack Heppner, to quote from his document "Reflections on Bolivian Mennonite Realities".
4. Permission from Abram G. Janzen's son William, to quote his entire booklet: "Altester Johann M. Loeppky, 1882-1950. As I Remember Him."
5. Permission from Lisa Janzen, author of *An Opened Gate* to summarize parts of it.
6. Preservings—the Plett Foundations. Permission from the D.F. Plett Historical Research Foundation to quote from the translated works of Bishop Johann M. Loeppky (Preservings no. 26) as well as quotes from the writings of Isaak M. Dyck (Preservings no. 44)

REFERENCES

Royden Loewen and Steven M. Nolt, *Seeking Places of Peace* (Intercourse, PA: Good Books, 2012), 78-79, 95.

Verna Martens, *Beyond Our Wildest Dreams* (Winnipeg, MB: Art Bookbindery, 2007), 80-81.

Delbert F. Plett, Q.C. *OLD COLONY Mennonites in Canada 1875 to 2000* (Steinbach, MB: Crossway Publications Inc., 2001), 127-128.

Cameron Dueck, *Menno Moto A Journey Across the Americas in Search of My Mennonite Identity* (Windsor, ON: Biblioasis, 2020), 189, 251.

www.ingramcontent.com/pod-product-compliance
Lightning Source LLC
LaVergne TN
LVHW051103080426
835508LV00019B/2034